Brief
Couples Therapy
Homework Planner

Brief Couples Therapy Homework Planner

Gary M. Schultheis
Bill O'Hanlon
Steffanie O'Hanlon

John Wiley & Sons, Inc.

New York • Chichester • Weinheim • Brisbane • Singapore • Toronto

---

Note about Photocopy Rights

The publisher grants purchasers permission to reproduce handouts from this book for professional use with their clients.

ISBN 0471-29511-6

Acknowledgments

Thanks to Kelly Franklin for another chance to work with her. Thanks to Bill and Steffanie O'Hanlon for agreeing to co-author this book. Their creativity adds a dimension that I could never have brought to the book on my own. Thanks to my parents, Bill and Mary Ann, who have supported me even when I didn't make sense. And finally, thanks to my wife, Sandy, who is always there when I need her.

GMS

Thanks to Gary for his patience and inspiration. To Carol, Jennifer, and Kim. And most of all to Bill, for his love and devotion, particularly through the hard parts.

SO'H

Thanks to Gary for including me in the project (sorry for the challenge that I offer as a collaborator, this is number sixteen, so I'm used to my process). Kelly Franklin gave her continued enthusiasm and support. Thanks to those couples who have been trusting enough to let me in on their dilemmas and who have been open to trying out these concepts. To my brother Paul, best wishes on your journey to reclaim yourself and thank you. Special thanks to Steffanie for teaching me a lot about the noun and verb aspects of love and relationship. (I'm still working on those boundaries, okay?)

BO'H

Practice Planner Series Preface

The practice of psychotherapy has a dimension that did not exist 30, 20, or even 15 years ago—accountability. Treatment programs, public agencies, clinics, and even group and solo practitioners must now justify the treatment of patients to outside review entities that control the payment of fees. This development has resulted in an explosion of paperwork.

Clinicians must now document what has been done in treatment, what is planned for the future, and what the anticipated outcomes of the interventions are. The books and software in this Practice Planner series are designed to help practitioners fulfill these documentation requirements efficiently and professionally.

The Practice Planner series is growing rapidly. It now includes not only the original *Complete Psychotherapy Treatment Planner* and the *Child and Adolescent Psychotherapy Treatment Planner,* but also *Treatment Planners* targeted to specialty areas of practice, including: chemical dependency, the continuum of care, couples therapy, older adult treatment, employee assistance, pastoral counseling, and more.

In addition to the *Treatment Planners,* the series also includes *TheraScribe®: The Computerized Assistant to Psychotherapy Treatment Planning* and *TheraBiller™: The Computerized Mental Health Office Manager,* as well as adjunctive books, such as the *Brief Therapy, Chemical Dependence, Couples,* and *Child Homework Planners, The Psychotherapy Documentation Primer,* and *Clinical, Forensic, Child, Couples and Family,* and *Chemical Dependence Documentation Sourcebooks*—containing forms and resources to aid in mental health practice management. The goal of the series is to provide practitioners with the resources they need in order to provide high-quality care in the era of accountability—or, to put it simply, we seek to help you spend more time on patients, and less on paperwork.

ARTHUR E. JONGSMA, JR.
Grand Rapids, Michigan

Contents

Contents

SECTION II—General Issues/Values Conflicts for Couples 89

SECTION III—Specific Problem Areas for Couples 119

Contents

Introduction

While it is common for mental health practitioners to complain about the changes that managed care has forced them to make in their work, we applaud one change that we believe is irreversible. It is now expected that therapy produce clear results, usually in a relatively short time. This expectation has forced therapists to become both more flexible and more creative in their practice. Homework assignments are becoming more and more attractive to practitioners as a way to facilitate change, regardless of their therapeutic approach. Homework expands on work done in a session and allows clients to take what has been discussed in therapy and try it in the real world. We hope that this book will be helpful to those who are just learning to use homework assignments. In addition, it offers some new ideas to those who are experienced with homework but want to expand their use of this technique.

Brief therapy is especially appropriate for couples work. Most couples seek therapy only when their relationship is in serious trouble. If we don't offer help and activities to make some rapid changes, there is often no relationship left to work with.

We use homework assignments for many reasons, including that homework:

- Introduces change to the situation
- Encourages a spirit of experimentation
- Encourages clients to take an active part in therapy
- Evokes resources
- Highlights and allows follow-through on something that happened in the session
- Encourages the client to put more attention on an issue
- Encourages the client to take the next step before the next session
- Enhances the client's search for solutions

How to Use This Book

This book is designed so that assignments can be easily copied from the disk and handed to clients. Many therapists work in situations where they don't have the luxury of time for creativity. This book will help fill the gaps caused by an overloaded schedule. While this is a legitimate way to use the book, we hope these assignments serve as a springboard of inspiration, encouraging therapists and clients to customize and create their own assignments. To make

1

this process easier, we are providing a disk with the forms that you can load on your computer and easily customize.

Years ago, we read a story about the rock star Sting, who brought some songs he had just written to his two fellow band members. "Take these home and make them your own," he told them. When the band members were done, the song sounded better than when Sting had first written it. This is our model. Change things around and make the assignment your own. Delete questions you don't like. Work the couple's language and metaphors into the assignment. Rewrite the introductory paragraph. Invite your clients to help you. Don't forget to have fun (at least some of the time).

This is not a self-help book, a one-size-fits-all approach. These tasks are not appropriate for everyone. Use your judgment about whether an assignment is appropriate for any given situation. To assist you, these assignments are also cross-referenced with *The Couples Psychotherapy Treatment Planner* (O'Lears, Heyman, & Jongsma, John Wiley & Sons, 1998). Use your experience and personal expertise to guide you.

We have also included some introductory material detailing the model we chose to generate these homework assignments. More details and examples of the model can be found in some of our previous writings on relationships (Hudson & O'Hanlon, 1991; O'Hanlon & Hudson, 1996; O'Hanlon & O'Hanlon, 1998).

We have also included some brochures that you can copy, personalize, and distribute to your clients. Feel free to modify these or generate your own. The more personalized you can make the hand-outs, the more participation you can expect from your clients.

ASSIGNING TASKS

It may be best to call these assignments tasks or experiments, not homework. That phrase evokes memories of meaningless activities handed out in school as busywork. Making the assignments relevant for clients is the way to ensure their cooperation. Task assignments are designed to bring about changes. We first make sure that we understand what the problem is that the client wants to change. By collaboratively designing tasks, we ensure that the assignments are relevant to the client. When the tasks are derived from a collaborative relationship, they are owned by both the practitioner and the client, that is, they are not "tasks" at all. Finally, we leave the client the option of discontinuing the assignment if he or she feels that it is in their best interest.

We have several ways to collaboratively design tasks. We offer clients multiple choice possibilities and suggestions when presenting suggested actions. In addition, we provide clients with a preview of responses to similar assignments. During this process, we closely observe the clients' reactions. If a client shakes his or her head adamantly during such a preview or starts to shift uncomfortably, we consider that this might not be the best task for this particular client. Likewise, if a client is smiling or nodding or leaning forward, we know we are probably on the right track.

One therapist, Steffanie, saw a family that had been referred to her by their pediatrician because their 10-year-old son, Larry, had been having escalating temper tantrums since his surgery for severe colitis. The family had never been to therapy; however, they settled in quickly and readily discussed their son's colitis and temper tantrums. Steffanie reassured them about the likelihood of solving the problem and proceeded to tell them stories. She also provided examples of tasks that had worked for other families. The father began to shift in his chair and occasionally sigh as Steffanie spoke about these interventions. After observing this behavior, Steffanie turned to the father and said, "I think I'm off target in some way. I notice you seem uncomfortable when I start to talk about things to do." The father said, "You're telling us things *we* can do to stop the tantrums. We thought if we brought him here, *you* could work with him to stop the tantrums."

Steffanie and the family discussed psychotherapy. Steffanie presented her ideas and explained that she preferred to involve the family in making changes. After all, the family (i.e., parents and siblings) was really the expert on their kids. She pointed out that they would be around when most of the tantrums occurred. Both parents seemed relieved and the mother confided that they felt responsible for missing the warning signs of their son's illness and were scared to "do anything wrong again." They had come to mistrust their judgment and think "the professionals knew better." The family felt newly empowered to take control of the situation. They worked with Steffanie on developing new strategies for effectively dealing with tantrums.

DEBRIEFING

An essential part of using homework assignments is *debriefing* after the assignment has been carried out. Did the task make things better or worse? What did the client learn? Were there any problems? For us, this is the stuff of treatment. The feedback we receive from the assignment frequently creates the direction of the session. For instance, a therapist told a couple having fights regarding money about another couple he had worked with who had made a commitment to trying weekly budget "summits" at which they would make joint decisions about household expenditures. This couple agreed to do the task, but when they returned, they reported that it hadn't worked. In the ensuing discussion, the wife said, "He out talks me every time and gets his way because he's better at arguing. He's like a lawyer and makes a forceful and persuasive case, I don't represent my side well." Knowing that, the therapist was able to help the couple hash out new ground rules for discussions that enabled them both to be heard and represented. This not only helped with the money discussions, but with other areas of difficulty they were having. Sometimes the brief therapy is criticized as "Band-Aid" therapy that doesn't deal with the "real problem." On the contrary, we often find that when clients enhance their problem-solving skills during brief therapy, they can generalize those skills to other contexts.

We often tell our clients that the tasks are experiments. This has several advantages. One unspoken message is that we don't have the answers. Framing the exercise as an experiment implies that the therapist isn't expecting it to be the final truth about what will work. In this way, the therapist encourages and models flexibility and attention to results. When the client performs an exercise, things either improve or they don't. Either way, both clients and therapists get important information that can inform the next action to be taken. Sometimes clients ask why we have designed an assignment in a particular way. We answer them as honestly as possible.

Another way we have found to increase the likelihood of follow through is to write the assignment down and follow up. We keep duplicate task forms so that we can give the client one copy, and keep the other to refer to at the next session. Thus, clients have something concrete to refer to between sessions. It also makes us more likely to remember to follow up with clients the next session. Following up is very important: It communicates to the clients that the assignment wasn't just dreamed up to test their compliance.

When we first started to use homework assignments, we didn't get as much compliance as we do now. Because we were unsure if our clients would follow through, we sent them ambivalent messages about our expectations. Now, we assume clients will do the tasks and our language reflects this: "*After* you do this, I will want to follow up on how it went," rather than, "*If* you do this, let me know how it went." This simple step of presupposing the client will comply has made a dramatic difference. If clients do not do the assignment between sessions, we don't automatically assume they are being resistant. We discuss the assignment and ask what happened. Often we discover the assignment was not clear enough, didn't fit, or clients have had a busy or overwhelming week.

When tasks are habitually not done, we use this analogy with clients: "I keep firing the starting pistol but you haven't left the blocks yet. You say you want to reach the finish line (your goal of fighting less, having more sex, doing better co-parenting, etc.), but you're still at the starting position looking at me as if to say, 'Why aren't we at the finish line yet?' The task we discussed is the starting pistol. Actions get you off the blocks and to the finish line."

When clients say they just don't have time or doing the task isn't a priority, we talk to them about whether they are motivated to work on the problem now and suggest they might want to return to therapy when they have the time and energy to focus on it. We have a general operating principal: The therapist should never be the most motivated person in the room. If you are more motivated than your clients, the whole therapy process will probably fail. Bill saw a sign in a restaurant once: Never try to teach a pig to sing, it wastes your time and annoys the pig! Perhaps you are trying to get people to do things that aren't right for them. You have an agenda for them that they are not motivated to fulfill. That is a no-win situation for you and your clients.

Section I

Generic Tasks

Introduction to Generic Tasks

This section gives general interventions that can be helpful across many problem areas. The next section provides assignments for specific problem areas. Because this book is mostly about getting people to do things that change relationships, we want to make a brief note about the importance of listening and acknowledging in this approach. In brief couples therapy, our initial goal is to help each partner feel heard, understood, and validated without taking sides or deciding who is right or wrong. This is the validation part of therapy. Couples often enter therapy feeling blamed or discouraged. Our first task is to help them feel that their feelings and points of view, even if they are negative, are legitimate and understandable. At the same time, we have to be careful not to take sides or decide who is right while we are validating. And we must not communicate the idea that the situation is set in concrete. We want to, at the very least, create some sense that the situation is not hopeless. That means we quickly move into making changes. So, in addition to validating, we immediately set about helping the couple make changes in three areas around the problem:

1. What they are paying attention to in the problem situation and how they are interpreting it? *(Changing the Viewing)*
2. How are they typically interacting with one another, including patterns of how each of them act during the problem situation and how they talk with one another or others about the problem? We are searching for repeating patterns and helping couples change those problem patterns. *(Changing the Doing)*
3. What circumstances surround the problem? That is, what are the family backgrounds and patterns, the cultural backgrounds and patterns, the racial backgrounds and gender training and experiences that are contributing to the problem? In what locations do the couple's problems usually happen? *(Changing the Context)*

In each of these change areas, we have two tasks:

1. Recognizing and interrupting typical problem patterns
2. Seeking, highlighting and encouraging solution patterns

6

When couples first enter therapy, they are typically focused on what is wrong and the problem parts of their situation. So we meet them there. But very early in the process of couples counseling, we also steer them toward telling us about times that have been better, moments when they solved the problems they were facing, incidents in which they were pleasantly surprised by their partner, or found unexpected compassion or kindness during a stressful conflict. Most couples do not spontaneously report or even remember these "solution moments," but once prompted, can recall and describe these solutions so that they become available for problem solving in the current situation. If a couple cannot identify solution moments, we might explore the ways that they have kept things from getting even worse than they are.

The following chart summarizes the three areas we focus our homework assignments on in couples therapy:

Areas for Intervention in Brief Couples Therapy

Viewing	Doing	Context
• Points of view • Attentional patterns • Interpretations • Explanations • Evaluations • Assumptions • Beliefs • Identity stories	• Action patterns • Interactional patterns • Language patterns • Nonverbal patterns	• Time patterns • Physical environment/spatial location • Cultural/racial background and propensities • Family/historical background and propensities • Biochemical/genetic background and propensities • Gender training and propensities • Connections to others • Spirituality
Challenge problem views that: *Blame* *Suggest that change is impossible* *Invalidate the person* *Suggest the person has no choice about his or her actions.* Offer new possibilities for attention.	Find patterns that are part of the problem and that repeat. Suggest disrupting the problematic patterns or find and use solution patterns.	Suggest shifts in the context around the problem (e.g., changes in biochemistry, time, space, cultural habits and influences). Use these areas to normalize (and therefore value and validate) as well as to find the problem and solution patterns in any or all of the contextual factors.

In brief couples therapy, we typically do not focus on historical issues or traumas that give rise to the couples' current difficulties. We focus more on the immediate problems that the couple are experiencing and help them make changes in those areas. The tasks that follow are congruent with this straightforward view of couples therapy but can be used with therapists of any theoretical orientation.

Chart Your Course

GOALS OF THE EXERCISE

1. To encourage the couple to clarify what they want.
2. To suggest that the couple focus on the goal of therapy rather than focusing so much on the problem.

TYPES OF PROBLEMS THIS EXERCISE MAY BE MOST USEFUL FOR

- Disillusionment with Relationship
- Infidelity
- Jealousy
- Life-Changing Events
- Loss of Love/Affection
- Midlife Crisis
- Personality Differences
- Separation and Divorce

SUGGESTIONS FOR PROCESSING THIS EXERCISE WITH THE COUPLE

1. How will you know therapy has been successful?
2. What will be or what has been the first sign of change?
3. What will you do to encourage change to continue?

CHART YOUR COURSE

Aimless wandering can be an enjoyable and sometimes profitable activity; however, if you want to accomplish something, you'll probably find that it's best not to count on serendipity to save the day. Pilots are required to file a flight plan before taking off. Lenders require a business plan before they lend money. If you haven't defined goals for your relationship recently, you may find this exercise helpful in getting you started making the changes you are looking for.

Between now and your next session, make a list of the things you would like to change in your relationship.

1. _____

2. _____

3. _____

4. _____

5. _____

6. _____

7. _____

8. _____

9. _____

10. _____

When you are finished with counseling, what will be different that will make you able to look back on the things you wanted to change and say to yourself, "Getting into counseling and doing the work I did there was one of the best things I've ever done for myself and my relationship"?

_____

_____

_____

_____

What will be or perhaps has been the first and smallest sign that change is beginning?

_____

_____

_____

_____

When you notice that first change, what can you do to keep the ball rolling?

_____

_____

_____

_____

Remember to bring completed work sheet to your next appointment.

Taking Charge of Change

GOALS OF THE EXERCISE

1. To get each partner to start taking responsibility for making changes rather than waiting for the other person to change.
2. To communicate the idea that one person can change a relationship.

TYPES OF PROBLEMS THIS EXERCISE MAY BE MOST USEFUL FOR

- Communication
- Dependency
- Disillusionment with Relationship
- Infidelity
- Life-Changing Events
- Loss of Love/Affection
- Midlife Crisis
- Personality Differences
- Separation and Divorce
- Work/Home Role Strain

SUGGESTIONS FOR PROCESSING THIS EXERCISE WITH THE COUPLE

1. What were the things you noticed that you could have done differently?
2. Did you do anything differently as a result of completing this exercise?
3. What changed as a result of your completing this exercise?

TAKING CHARGE OF CHANGE

Even if the other person is, in your view, the source of the problem, there are things you can do to take back your power and to make a difference in the relationship. This exercise may help you find the places where you have some personal power.

Describe three situations that occur between now and your next session that are representative of something you would like to change in your relationship. In your description, focus on what you do or experience in the situation rather than how you want the other person to change. Pay special attention to things that you may say or do, rather than what your partner does. Note how you respond to your partner. Write your description as objectively as possible, as if you are an uninvolved third party. After you write your description, let it rest for a day. Then study it and look for as many things as possible that you might have done differently that would have changed the event. Be ready to discuss these ideas with your therapist in your next session.

Situation 1

What happened?

_____

_____

_____

_____

What could you have done differently?

_____

_____

_____

_____

Situation 2

What happened?

_____

_____

_____

What could you have done differently?

_____

_____

_____

Situation 3

What happened?

_____

_____

_____

What could you have done differently?

_____

_____

_____

Remember to bring completed work sheet to your next appointment.

Unpack Loaded and Vague Words

GOALS OF THE EXERCISE

1. To help move couples from vague or blaming communications to more specific and change-oriented talk.
2. To help you, the therapist, get a better picture of what is happening with the couple.

TYPES OF PROBLEMS THIS EXERCISE MAY BE MOST USEFUL FOR

- Anger
- Anxiety
- Blame
- Communication
- Dependency
- Intolerance
- Jealousy

SUGGESTIONS FOR PROCESSING THIS EXERCISE WITH THE COUPLE

1. How was this exercise helpful to you?
2. What did you learn that surprised you by doing this exercise?
3. How did it feel different using videotalk than your usual way of talking?

UNPACK LOADED AND VAGUE WORDS

Have you noticed that when you use certain words or phrases you can get a rise out of your partner? For example, you might find that when you say things like, "You're being selfish," or "You're just like your father," your partner reacts badly. You might think of these words as packaged words—*words and phrases that may mean something specific to you, but which have meanings that are not clear to your partner. It's often best to unpack those vague words and phrases and get specific. The simplest way to defuse such phrases and words is to translate them into action descriptions or what could be called* videotalk: *Use words that describe what you could see and hear on a videotape, rather than using more vague or judgmental words. So, instead of saying, "Well, when you were judging me, I got defensive." You could try saying, "When you pointed your finger at me and said I was immature, I got defensive." Instead of telling your partner that the problem is what he or she* is, *it is usually less threatening and more conducive to change to focus on what he or she* does *that is a problem for you. This exercise is designed to help you unpack your vague or provocatively labeled box.*

1. Think of three things that your partner does or has done recently that you don't like and list them below as you normally express them.

   _____

   _____

   _____

   _____

2. Translate each complaint to videotalk.

   _____

   _____

   _____

   _____

3. Find an appropriate time and, using videotalk, tell your partner the three things that he or she has done that you haven't liked. Do not give them your ideas about why they did it or a prediction about what they will do about it in the future. Avoid generalizing or labeling. Get specific about what it looked like and sounded like.

_____

_____

_____

_____

4. Invite your partner to tell you three things that you have done that he or she hasn't liked.

_____

_____

_____

5. If they give you their theory or story about it or are vague, gently steer them back to getting specific with videotalk by suggesting that you really want to know what they would like you to change.

_____

_____

_____

_____

6. Write your partner's complaints in videotalk.

_____

_____

_____

_____

7. How did videotalk change your interaction?

_____

_____

_____

_____

8. What, if anything, was difficult for you about using videotalk?

_____

_____

_____

_____

9. Do you have any objection to using videotalk in the future?

_____

_____

_____

_____

Remember to bring completed work sheet to your next appointment.

Doing Love and Intimacy

GOALS OF THE EXERCISE

1. To get couples to begin to act in more kind and loving ways to one another.
2. To communicate the idea that feelings can change and be affected by actions.

TYPES OF PROBLEMS THIS EXERCISE MAY BE MOST USEFUL FOR

- Anger
- Communication
- Disillusionment with Relationship
- Infidelity
- Intolerance
- Jealousy
- Loss of Love/Affection
- Midlife Crisis
- Personality Difference
- Separation and Divorce
- Sexual Dysfunction

SUGGESTIONS FOR PROCESSING THIS EXERCISE WITH THE COUPLE

1. Did you feel more loving as you did more loving things?
2. Did your partner seem more loving to you?
3. How could you use what you learned from doing this exercise in the future in your relationship?

DOING LOVE AND INTIMACY

> *Sometimes people are waiting for the feelings they used to have to come back. Another approach that sometimes works better is to take action even if you don't feel like it to see what feelings arise. If you are not feeling love or intimacy right now, examine how loving and intimately you are behaving. Try acting loving for a period of time and find out if you start to feel more love.*

1. Write in detail, five things you would do if you were in a relationship in which you were really in love with your partner. For the purpose of this exercise, make it five things that do not depend on the active participation of your partner.

    _____

    _____

    _____

    _____

    _____

2. For the next two weeks, do any of those five things each day in relationship with your partner. If you get ideas for more than five things, feel free to add those things to your repertoire of behaviors. Record your experience below for each day.

Day 1

What did you do?

_____

_____

What did you learn?

_____

_____

Day 2

What did you do?

_____

_____

What did you learn?

_____

_____

Day 3

What did you do?

_____

_____

What did you learn?

_____

_____

Day 4

What did you do?

_____

_____

What did you learn?

_____

_____

Day 5

What did you do?

_____

_____

What did you learn?

_____

_____

Day 6

What did you do?

_____

_____

What did you learn?

_____

_____

Day 7

What did you do?

_____

_____

What did you learn?

_____

_____

Day 8

What did you do?

_____

_____

What did you learn?

_____

_____

Day 9

What did you do?

_____

_____

What did you learn?

_____

_____

Day 10

What did you do?

_____

_____

What did you learn?

_____

_____

Day 11

What did you do?

_____

_____

What did you learn?

_____

_____

Day 12

What did you do?

_____

_____

What did you learn?

_____

_____

Day 13

What did you do?

_____

_____

What did you learn?

_____

_____

Day 14

What did you do?

_____

_____

What did you learn?

_____

_____

Remember to bring completed work sheet to your next appointment.

Track the Problems and Solutions

GOALS OF THE EXERCISE

1. To get a reading on the severity of the couple's problems.
2. To communicate the awareness that problems are not constant and can change in intensity, severity, and frequency.

TYPES OF PROBLEMS THIS EXERCISE MAY BE MOST USEFUL FOR

- Anger
- Anxiety
- Blame
- Communication
- Depression
- Eating Disorder
- Financial Conflict
- Job Stress
- Parenting Conflicts

SUGGESTIONS FOR PROCESSING THIS EXERCISE WITH THE COUPLE

1. What did you two learn about what made the problem better or worse?
2. What days was the problem typically worse or better?
3. What could you do in the future with what you learned from this exercise to improve your relationship?

TRACK THE PROBLEMS AND SOLUTIONS

Every day brings the opportunity to learn from experience. If you pay attention only to your failures or problems, you may learn what not to do, but you miss many chances to go further in the directions that have been helpful. This is an exercise to help you become more aware of your success so you can put it to good use.

Choose a time each day to think about your situation. At that time, create an imaginary scale from 0 to 100 that ranges from the worst your situation could possibly be to absolute utopia (don't forget that utopia is translated "nowhere"). Now place yourself on that scale and write the number below. In the space below the graph, note anything that you have done that has helped you or your relationship. If you are feeling down today, note what you have done that kept things from getting even worse. If two of you are doing this exercise, realize that your partner will be likely to have a different way of looking at the situation and there is no reason why your experiences have to match. Note on the back of the page how the two of you handle differences in your experiences.

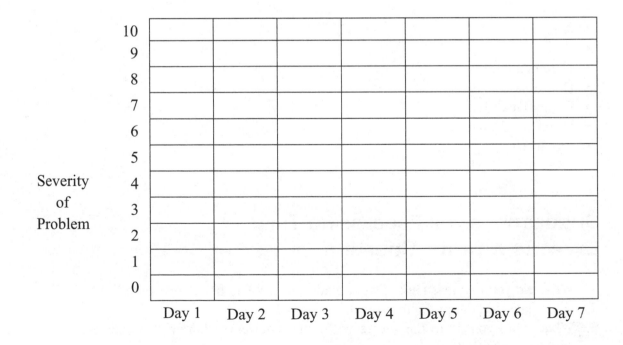

Remember to bring completed work sheet to your next appointment.

Identify and Validate Your Partner's Feelings and Points of View

GOALS OF THE EXERCISE

1. To help the couple listen to and stop blaming one another.
2. To clarify miscommunications and misunderstandings.

TYPES OF PROBLEMS THIS EXERCISE MAY BE MOST USEFUL FOR

- Communication
- Financial Conflict
- Jealousy
- Job Stress
- Life-Changing Events
- Midlife Crisis
- Religion/Spirituality Differences
- Work/Home Role Strain

SUGGESTIONS FOR PROCESSING THIS EXERCISE WITH THE COUPLE

1. How did it feel for you to be listened to and validated?
2. How did it feel to listen and validate?
3. What surprised you in doing this exercise?

IDENTIFY AND VALIDATE YOUR PARTNER'S FEELINGS AND POINTS OF VIEW

> *Sometimes the simplest solution is to just stop and listen to what your partner is saying and imagine how he or she could be feeling that way or seeing things in that light.*

Try this experiment between now and your next session. Choose three situations when your partner is complaining about you or something you did. Don't try to defend yourself, correct his perceptions, or talk him out of his feelings. Just put yourself in his position and try to hear how he understands, interprets, and feels about the situation and imagine how you would feel or act if you were seeing things that way. (If what he or she is saying sounds crazy or unreasonable, consider the possibility that you are missing something and listen more to see if you can understand.) Express that understanding and let him know how difficult it must be for him, given how he is feeling about the situation.

Record your experiences below for each situation:

_____

_____

_____

_____

_____

_____

_____

_____

1. What was your partner's complaint?

_____

_____

_____

_____

_____

2. What did you learn by listening?

_____

_____

_____

_____

_____

3. How did changing your behavior affect the interaction?

_____

_____

_____

_____

_____

Remember to bring completed work sheet to your next appointment.

Changing Character Indictments to Action Descriptions

GOALS OF THE EXERCISE

1. To help couples change their unproductive criticism and conflict patterns.
2. To help couples get specific in their complaints in order to make the possibility of change more likely.

TYPES OF PROBLEMS THIS EXERCISE MAY BE MOST USEFUL FOR

- Blended-Family Problems
- Communication
- Financial Conflict
- Jealousy
- Job Stress
- Life-Changing Events
- Midlife Crisis
- Religion/Spirituality Differences
- Work/Home Role Strain

SUGGESTIONS FOR PROCESSING THIS EXERCISE WITH THE COUPLE

1. How did this descriptive process feel different to you?
2. Did you get any new ideas about your partner from doing this exercise?
3. Did you notice anything that improved resulting from this exercise?

CHANGING CHARACTER INDICTMENTS TO ACTION DESCRIPTIONS

> *It's very difficult to build bridges at the same time that you are building walls. If you attack another person verbally, you can expect them to put up a defense, which can make communication difficult. When you want to talk about something someone did that upset you, try talking about the behavior rather than about the person's character or something else that is very difficult for them to change.*

Each time you find yourself in a situation where you would customarily lash out about your partner's flaws, rather than proceed as usual, substitute a description of the behavior you object to. Stick to a factual description of what happened and explain clearly what you would like them to do instead.

Record the incident. Then write a clear description of exactly what happened. Stick to things that you can see and hear in your description.

Date: _____ Time: _____

Place: _____

Describe the behavior that you objected to:

_____

_____

_____

_____

_____

_____

_____

What did you say?

_____

_____

_____

What difference do you think that your change in language made?

_____

_____

_____

Date: _____ Time: _____

Place: _____

Describe the behavior that you objected to:

_____

_____

_____

What did you say?

_____

_____

_____

What difference do you think that your change in language made?

_____

_____

_____

Remember to bring completed work sheet to your next appointment.

Identify What Has Worked and Do More of That

GOALS OF THE EXERCISE

1. To invite couples to look at a problem in more detail with an eye toward finding solutions.
2. To further suggest that each partner may be able to affect the problem.

TYPES OF PROBLEMS THIS EXERCISE MAY BE MOST USEFUL FOR

- Anger
- Blame
- Communication
- Dependency
- Life-Changing Events
- Parenting Conflicts
- Recreational Activities Dispute
- Sexual Dysfunction
- Work/Home Role Strain

SUGGESTIONS FOR PROCESSING THIS EXERCISE WITH THE COUPLE

1. When was the problem less serious?
2. What did you do to influence the problem?
3. What did you learn from this exercise?

IDENTIFY WHAT HAS WORKED AND DO MORE OF THAT

> *One way to solve problems is to look at what you are already doing that works and do it more. The difficulty is that unless you are looking for the successes, especially the small ones, they can go unnoticed. Chances are that you know more than you think you do.*

Identify ten things that you and your partner do well. For each of the ten things, identify three skills that are used in that behavior.

1. _____

    Skills: _____

    _____

    _____

2. _____

    Skills: _____

    _____

    _____

3. _____

    Skills: _____

    _____

    _____

4. _____

    Skills: _____

    _____

    _____

5. _____

Skills: _____

_____

_____

6. _____

Skills: _____

_____

_____

7. _____

Skills: _____

_____

_____

8. _____

Skills: _____

_____

_____

9. _____

Skills: _____

_____

_____

10. _____

Skills: _____

_____

_____

Consider the skills that you demonstrate and identify any that might help you in situations where you have been having difficulty.

Remember to bring completed work sheet to your next appointment.

Little Things Mean a Lot

GOALS OF THE EXERCISE

1. To get couples to notice that there are aspects of their relationship that are fine.
2. To reorient the couple's attention to the parts of their relationship that are working rather than those that are problematic.

TYPES OF PROBLEMS THIS EXERCISE MAY BE MOST USEFUL FOR

- Anger
- Anxiety
- Blended-Family Problems
- Depression
- Disillusionment with Relationship
- Loss of Love/Affection
- Religion/Spirituality Differences
- Separation and Divorce
- Sexual Dysfunction

SUGGESTIONS FOR PROCESSING THIS EXERCISE WITH THE COUPLE

1. Were you surprised that there were some aspects of your relationship that you didn't want to change or that were working fine?
2. How did focusing on those aspects change your view of or feelings about the relationship?
3. Did you get any ideas for things you might be able to do to change your relationship for the better through doing this exercise?

36

LITTLE THINGS MEAN A LOT

> *Each day note below three things regarding the problem situation that you do NOT want to change. Notice times when you and your partner handle a situation well or at least better than you expected. Note your part in making these things happen or continue to happen.*

Day 1

1. _____
2. _____
3. _____

Day 2

1. _____
2. _____
3. _____

Day 3

1. _____
2. _____
3. _____

Day 4

1. _____
2. _____
3. _____

Day 5

1. _____

2. _____

3. _____

Day 6

1. _____

2. _____

3. _____

Day 7

1. _____

2. _____

3. _____

Remember to bring completed work sheet to your next appointment.

Keep One Eye on the Road

GOALS OF THE EXERCISE

1. To get couples oriented to change rather than how they are stuck.
2. To get couples to notice and acknowledge small signs of progress rather than focusing on having to see big changes to feel hopeful or better about the relationship.

TYPES OF PROBLEMS THIS EXERCISE MAY BE MOST USEFUL FOR

- Alcohol Abuse
- Blame
- Dependency
- Depression
- Eating Disorder
- Physical Abuse
- Psychological Abuse
- Sexual Abuse

SUGGESTIONS FOR PROCESSING THIS EXERCISE WITH THE COUPLE

1. Was thinking about what you wanted to have happen and noticing any small steps towards that helpful?
2. Was thinking about what you want more helpful than thinking about all the things you don't want or haven't liked.
3. What little signs did you notice that were good signs?

KEEP ONE EYE ON THE ROAD

One of the hazards of being a photographer is what can happen to you if you start walking while you look through your camera. This can be tragic if you are someplace like the Grand Canyon. While less dramatic, there are dangers in failing to see what's right in front of you in everyday life. If you want changes in your relationship and you fail to see and acknowledge small successes or improvements, you run the risk of squelching change before it gets a good start. This exercise will help you learn to watch for those little signs of movement that can become monumental.

1. Describe what you want to happen.

   _____

   _____

   _____

2. Write at least five things that would represent movement toward your goal.

   _____

   _____

   _____

   _____

   _____

3. Between now and your next session, note anything that happens that you see as a step in the right direction and be ready to discuss how it came about.

   _____

   _____

   _____

   _____

Remember to bring completed work sheet to your next appointment.

Time Travel

GOALS OF THE EXERCISE

1. To get the couple thinking in terms of solution rather than in terms of problem.
2. To get the couple focused more on the future and present than on the past.

TYPES OF PROBLEMS THIS EXERCISE MAY BE MOST USEFUL FOR

- Anger
- Blame
- Communication
- Dependency
- Infidelity
- Life-Changing Events
- Midlife Crisis

SUGGESTIONS FOR PROCESSING THIS EXERCISE WITH THE COUPLE

1. What were your five actions that would lead to that preferred future?
2. What three changes in thinking would you make if that were your future?
3. What did you learn from doing this exercise?

<u>**TIME TRAVEL**</u>

This exercise involves imagining that a problem is solved and describing what is different in that future. It is a bit like riding in a backward-facing seat in a train. You get an entirely different view than if you are facing forward. Strangely, this can get your mindset out of the problem and into thinking about solutions. Then you can work backwards from this solution future to the present with this new mindset.

1. Imagine that the relationship problem or problems you've been struggling with are resolved. Things worked out well for both of you. Nobody lost. This might take some imagination, but do your best. After you've imagined yourself in that place for a while, write a detailed description of your life and your relationship in that place where the problem is solved.

   _____

   _____

2. Write five things that would you do or say differently right now if you knew for certain that you are headed toward that future?

   _____

   _____

   _____

   _____

   _____

3. List three things you would think about differently right now if you knew for an absolute fact that you were headed toward that future?

   _____

   _____

   _____

4. What effect would it have if you started doing those things even though the outcome is uncertain?

_____

_____

_____

_____

5. What adjustments will you have to make to start doing those things knowing that there are no guarantees of success?

_____

_____

_____

_____

Remember to bring completed work sheet to your next appointment.

What Is Your Map of Love-Land?

GOALS OF THE EXERCISE

1. To get couples to realize that they often have different definitions and criteria for love and affection.
2. To help couples teach one another about those differences.

TYPES OF PROBLEMS THIS EXERCISE MAY BE MOST USEFUL FOR

- Communication
- Dependency
- Disillusionment with Relationship
- Infidelity
- Jealousy
- Loss of Love/Affection
- Personality Differences

SUGGESTIONS FOR PROCESSING THIS EXERCISE WITH THE COUPLE

1. What surprised you about what your partner said or wrote?
2. What did you learn about yourself from doing this?
3. How will doing this exercise change your relationship?

WHAT IS YOUR MAP OF LOVE-LAND?

We all have our own ideas about what constitutes a loving relationship. This can cause problems when one person is putting forth an effort but because of the expectations the other has, the effort doesn't get acknowledged. The only way you can be certain of someone else's desires is if they communicate them some way. The purpose of this exercise is to facilitate communication of your expectations so that in the future you will both be aware of what the other person is looking for. One caution is that all maps change over time, so you might want to plan now for when you will make revisions. An outdated map can be as bad as no map at all.

Give three examples of your idea of a romantic evening.

_____

_____

_____

List the three most romantic times the two of you have enjoyed together.

_____

_____

_____

What are three things you like to do together that cost no money?

_____

_____

_____

When have you felt most loved in the past three years?

_____

_____

_____

When have you felt closest in your relationship?

_____

_____

_____

When have you felt most valued in the past three years?

_____

_____

_____

What are five things partners do to communicate that they care about each other?

_____

_____

_____

_____

_____

Find an appropriate time to share this information with your partner and invite him or her to let you see their "map."

_____

_____

_____

Remember to bring completed work sheet to your next appointment.

Acknowledgment

GOALS OF THE EXERCISE

1. To move couples from blaming and misunderstanding one another into listening to and acknowledging their partner's feelings and points of view.
2. To give each person an experience of being heard.

TYPES OF PROBLEMS THIS EXERCISE MAY BE MOST USEFUL FOR

- Blame
- Communication
- Jealousy
- Life-Changing Events
- Midlife Crisis
- Religion/Spirituality Differences
- Work/Home Role Strain

SUGGESTIONS FOR PROCESSING THIS EXERCISE WITH THE COUPLE

1. How was being acknowledged different from your usual conversations or interactions?
2. What did each of you learn from this exercise?
3. What do you plan to do differently in the future since you have done this exercise?

ACKNOWLEDGMENT

> *Often when conversations get stuck, it's because both participants are paying more attention to what they are saying than what the other person is saying. Messages that are sent out but never acknowledged tend to get repeated and repeated louder and faster. Simply acknowledging the point the other is making lets him or her know that you were listening and increases the chance of listening on the part of the other.*

At least once a day repeat the feeling or point of view that your partner is telling you before you express your point. Keep restating it until the partner agrees that you have correctly reflected what is going on for them. You might want to use the phrase "Let me make sure I understand you" or "So, you're saying …" Record your results below. Copy this sheet to add more days.

Day 1

What point did you acknowledge?

_____

_____

What was the result of your action?

_____

_____

Day 2

What point did you acknowledge?

_____

_____

What was the result of your action?

_____

_____

Remember to bring completed work sheet to your next appointment.

Catch Your Partner Doing Something Right

GOALS OF THE EXERCISE

1. To change the couples patterns of attention and talk from blame to praise and credit.
2. To give you, the therapist, information about what is going well in the couple's relationship.

TYPES OF PROBLEMS THIS EXERCISE MAY BE MOST USEFUL FOR

- Anger
- Blame
- Blended-Family Problems
- Communication
- Financial Conflict
- Job Stress
- Sexual Dysfunction
- Work/Home Role Strain

SUGGESTIONS FOR PROCESSING THIS EXERCISE WITH THE COUPLE

1. How did your partner respond when you gave him or her credit?
2. What surprised you about his or her response to getting credit?
3. How will this change your interactions or relationship?

49

CATCH YOUR PARTNER DOING SOMETHING RIGHT

Most of us are good at noticing when someone steps on our toes, but we are unaware of how often they go out of their way to avoid doing so. Letting others know when we like what they do is a way of acknowledging behavior, as well as teaching them our preferences. This exercise will help you develop your ability to be aware of your partner's efforts.

Between now and your next session, at least twice a day, make a note of something your partner does that helps your relationship. When possible, find an appropriate way to let your partner know that you appreciate the effort. Watch for times when you felt cared about, helped, or understood and try to identify specific things that led you to feel that way. (*Hint:* You can also catch yourself doing something right and silently give yourself credit. Notice when you are being flexible, compassionate, and understanding.) Record what you acknowledged and the response of your partner.

Day 1

What did you acknowledge or give your partner credit for?

_____

How did your partner respond?

_____

Day 2

What did you acknowledge or give your partner credit for?

_____

How did your partner respond?

_____

Day 3

What did you acknowledge or give your partner credit for?

_____

How did your partner respond?

_____

Day 4

What did you acknowledge or give your partner credit for?

_____

How did your partner respond?

_____

Day 5

What did you acknowledge or give your partner credit for?

_____

How did your partner respond?

_____

Day 6

What did you acknowledge or give your partner credit for?

_____

How did your partner respond?

_____

Day 7

What did you acknowledge or give your partner credit for?

_____

How did your partner respond?

_____

Remember to bring completed work sheet to your next appointment.

51

Let Your Partner Know
What Behaviors You'd Like

GOALS OF THE EXERCISE

1. To get couples to begin to focus on what they want rather than what they don't want.
2. To move the discussion into action talk and away from blaming or vague talk.

TYPES OF PROBLEMS THIS EXERCISE MAY BE MOST USEFUL FOR

- Anger
- Blame
- Communication
- Dependency
- Depression
- Jealousy
- Life-Changing Events
- Sexual Dysfunction

SUGGESTIONS FOR PROCESSING THIS EXERCISE WITH THE COUPLE

1. Did anything change as a result of your doing this exercise?
2. Did you discuss your list with your partner?
3. What did you learn from doing this exercise?

LET YOUR PARTNER KNOW WHAT BEHAVIORS YOU'D LIKE

It is usually easy for most of us to identify things that we don't like or that cause us pain. While this is a very valuable survival skill, we often focus on that side of things to the detriment of the things that we like or prefer. Identifying and asking for actions that you'd like the other person to start doing or do more of can have a dramatic effect on behavior, especially in situations that involve others. Remember to focus on actions the other person could do, not on changes to their personality or on asking them to give up or alter their feelings.

Make a list of at least three actions, relevant to the problem you are working on, that you would like the other person to start doing or do more often. Be as specific and clear as possible. Direct your attention to *actions* rather than personality traits or characteristics. You may want to think in terms of small steps in the right direction. Add to your list as time passes between now and your next session. For your next session, be prepared to discuss how you might best use this information.

_____

_____

_____

_____

_____

_____

_____

_____

Remember to bring completed work sheet to your next appointment.

Just the Facts, Ma'am

GOALS OF THE EXERCISE

1. To help couples separate their interpretations and projections from what is actually happening in the relationship.
2. To get couples talking about their interpretations and checking them out with one another.

TYPES OF PROBLEMS THIS EXERCISE MAY BE MOST USEFUL FOR

- Anger
- Blame
- Communication
- Intolerance
- Jealousy
- Loss of Love/Affection

SUGGESTIONS FOR PROCESSING THIS EXERCISE WITH THE COUPLE

1. What surprised you most about your partner's interpretations and stories?
2. Did you notice any patterns in your stories?
3. If so, where, when or how do you think these patterns arose?

JUST THE FACTS MA'AM

> *We make interpretations or stories to help us understand life. But sometimes the stories we make are not helpful and are even the source of problems. One of the ways to challenge unhelpful stories is to separate one's story (interpretation) from what is actually happening (the facts, what you can see and hear). This is one way that you can be open to a new story or just stop getting stuck with the same unhelpful story.*

Think of a situation that you are unhappy about in your relationship. Describe what happens as if you could see it on a videotape or as if you were telling it to a Martian who didn't understand humans.

_____

_____

Now list the reasons why you think the other person did what they did or what this means that these things happened in your relationship. Aspects of stories we typically use:

Intentions: What do you think the person was trying to accomplish by doing the behavior?

Traits: What traits or characteristics do you think your partner was showing when doing the behavior?

The Past: What link to the past does this behavior have?

The Future: What does this say to you about the likely future of your relationship?

_____

_____

_____

The answers to these questions are the stories; they may be factual or they may be your own interpretations. Either way, it is good to check them out with your partner and not automatically assume they are true. You may find that you can put your stories "on the back burner" and deal only with the facts. Use the back of this page if you need more room.

Remember to bring completed work sheet to your next appointment.

Map the Problem

GOALS OF THE EXERCISE

1. To get couples to gather objective information for the therapist about the typical course and pattern of the problem.
2. To locate places to intervene in the pattern to change the problem.

TYPES OF PROBLEMS THIS EXERCISE MAY BE MOST USEFUL FOR

- Alcohol Abuse
- Anger
- Dependency
- Depression
- Eating Disorder
- Physical Abuse
- Psychological Abuse

SUGGESTIONS FOR PROCESSING THIS EXERCISE WITH THE COUPLE

1. Did you find that while you were gathering information about the problem, you came up with some ideas about how to change it?
2. What is one thing that each of you could do differently now that you have learned about the typical patterns of the problem?
3. If you were an engineer, could you redesign this problem so that it would lead to a solution or a better outcome?

MAP THE PROBLEM

This is an exercise in observation, both of yourself and your partner in the problem situation. Between now and your next session, observe yourself and your partner when the problem happens. Spell out as specifically as possible what typically happens when the problem occurs. The more details you include, the more helpful this exercise is likely to be. Take notes as the problem unfolds if you need to. It would be helpful for each person to do this exercise independently.

1. When does the problem usually happen?

   _____

   _____

2. When does the problem rarely happen?

   _____

   _____

3. Where does the problem usually happen?

   _____

   _____

4. When does the problem rarely happen?

   _____

   _____

5. Are there any other constants you can identify about when the problem happens and when it doesn't?

   _____

   _____

6. What is your first inkling that the problem is starting? Be specific about words, body language, actions, and voice.

_____

_____

7. How do you respond? Be specific about words, body language, actions, and voice.

_____

_____

8. What does your partner do? Be specific about words, body language, actions, and voice.

_____

_____

Write a detailed step-by-step account or draw a flowchart of how the problem typically unfolds. Use another sheet of paper if necessary.

Remember to bring completed work sheet to your next appointment.

Breaking Patterns

GOALS OF THE EXERCISE

1. To suggest that couples have some control over their situation.
2. To introduce some change into the situation.
3. To dissuade couples from attempting to change everything at once.

TYPES OF PROBLEMS THIS EXERCISE MAY BE MOST USEFUL FOR

- Alcohol Abuse
- Anger
- Blame
- Dependency
- Depression
- Eating Disorder
- Physical Abuse
- Psychological Abuse

SUGGESTIONS FOR PROCESSING THIS EXERCISE WITH THE COUPLE

1. What do you want to change?
2. What is it that you would rather be doing?
3. What did you learn by keeping your old behavior?
4. What did you learn on the days you tried something different?
5. What difference will this make?

BREAKING PATTERNS

One of the handy things that the human brain is able to do is to learn behaviors that can be used over and over. While this ability is great most of the time, it sometimes works against us. If you have learned a behavior pattern that no longer works and is causing you distress, you can often break away from it by using humor. Lighten up and get silly. For instance, instead of fighting, get water pistols, stand back to back, and walk out ten paces in opposite directions, turn and fire until the pistols are empty. Have a water balloon fight or pillow fight (light pillows or boppers).

Describe what you will do to break the pattern the next time you notice it.

_____

_____

After you have broken the pattern, answer the following questions:

Who noticed the pattern and what did you notice?

_____

_____

What would have happened if you had not done the exercise?

_____

_____

How did the exercise change things?

_____

_____

What did you learn from this that you can use in the future?

_____

_____

Remember to bring completed work sheet to your next appointment.

Don't Get Even, Get Odd

GOALS OF THE EXERCISE

1. To suggest that the client has some control over the situation.
2. To introduce some change into the situation.
3. To dissuade the client from changing everything at once.

TYPES OF PROBLEMS THIS EXERCISE MAY BE MOST USEFUL FOR

- Anger
- Anxiety
- Blame
- Blended-Family Problems
- Communication
- Dependency
- Depression Independent of Relationship Problems
- Depression Due to Relationship
- Work/Home Role Strain

SUGGESTIONS FOR PROCESSING THIS EXERCISE WITH THE COUPLE

1. What do you want to change?
2. What is it that you would rather be doing?
3. What did you learn by keeping your old behavior?
4. What did you learn on the days you tried something different?
5. What difference will this make?

DON'T GET EVEN, GET ODD

> *Sometimes when change is difficult, it can be helpful to learn a bit more about a behavior before changing it. Here is one way to do that. Write clearly the behavior you want to change.*

_____

_____

_____

What would you rather be doing?

_____

_____

On odd-numbered days (for example, the first and third of the month), do nothing different. Make those days exactly like the days you have been having. On even-numbered days, do the new behavior. For each day, answer the questions:

Odd Day 1: What did you do that was the same old thing?

Observations and Comments:

_____

_____

_____

Even Day 1: What did you do that was different?

Observations and Comments:

_____

_____

_____

Odd Day 2: What did you do that was the same old thing?

Observations and Comments:

_____

_____

Even Day 2: What did you do that was different?

Observations and Comments:

_____

_____

Odd Day 3: What did you do that was the same old thing?

Observations and Comments:

_____

_____

Even Day 3: What did you do that was different?

Observations and Comments:

_____

_____

Odd Day 4: What did you do that was the same old thing?

Observations and Comments:

_____

_____

Even Day 4: What did you do that was different?

Observations and Comments:

_____

_____

Odd Day 5: What did you do that was the same old thing?

Observations and Comments:

_____

_____

Even Day 5: What did you do that was different?

Observations and Comments:

_____

_____

Odd Day 6: What did you do that was the same old thing?

Observations and Comments:

_____

_____

Even Day 6: What did you do that was different?

Observations and Comments:

_____

_____

Odd Day 7: What did you do that was the same old thing?

Observations and Comments:

_____

_____

Even Day 7: What did you do that was different?

Observations and Comments:

_____

_____

Remember to bring completed work sheet to your next appointment.

Change the Context

GOALS OF THE EXERCISE

1. To give clients a sense that they can make a difference in their problem.
2. To raise awareness of spiritual and family/cultural background options and resources.

TYPES OF PROBLEMS THIS EXERCISE MAY BE MOST USEFUL FOR

- Blended-Family Problems
- Recreational Activities Dispute
- Religion/Spirituality Differences

SUGGESTIONS FOR PROCESSING THIS EXERCISE WITH THE COUPLE

1. Which one of these suggestions appealed to you the most? Why?
2. What changes came from doing this exercise?
3. Could you think of other things that weren't suggested in the exercise that are like the suggestions given here and that might be helpful?

CHANGE THE CONTEXT

> *Sometimes trying to directly change the situation leads to resistance and frustration. Coming through the side door rather than taking a frontal approach can lead to better results. In this exercise, we suggest you try changing anything that is in the context around the problem.*

This could include changing the timing of the problem, changing where it usually takes place, drawing on your spiritual resources, challenging your usual gender training (for example, women usually wait until the other person is done talking to speak, but men often interrupt). Below we provide a list of some of the variables and taken-for-granted aspects of your context that you could question, challenge, and change. Pick any of these that appeal to you and try it in the next week.

1. Notice and change the usual timing of the problem, that is, when it usually happens, how long it lasts, or its frequency. You might time your arguments and limit them to five minutes each. Take a break for five minutes and then start again for another five minutes. If you usually argue at night, make time in the early morning hours to argue. Record your actions and the results below.

   _____

   _____

   _____

2. Change the usual location for the problem or the spatial arrangement of your arguments or problems. One couple who couldn't stop arguing went into the bathroom. The man laid down in the bathtub and the woman sat on the toilet next to the bathtub. They ended up feeling so strange that they changed their arguing styles and were able to sort things out much better. Record your actions and the results below.

   _____

   _____

   _____

3. Identify your usual conflict patterns that you learned from the family in which you grew up and try some new ones. Some families never argue or raise their voices. Some families argue all the time and always raise their voices. Ask three of your friends to teach you the conflict resolution or avoidance patterns they learned from their families and practice using them in your relationship. Record your actions and the results below.

_____

_____

_____

4. In the middle of a conflict, get in touch with your spirituality in whatever way you are comfortable (praying, remembering that each person is a child of God, imagining your connection to Universal Love, having a sense that Jesus, Mohammed, Allah, Zoroaster, or Buddha is in the room with you). Proceed with the conflict with your spiritual resources leading the way. Record your actions and the results below.

_____

_____

_____

Remember to bring completed work sheet to your next appointment.

Negotiating Impasses

GOALS OF THE EXERCISE

1. To help couples learn or use negotiation skills.
2. To get couples through an impasse.

TYPES OF PROBLEMS THIS EXERCISE MAY BE MOST USEFUL FOR

- Blame
- Communication
- Personality Differences

SUGGESTIONS FOR PROCESSING THIS EXERCISE WITH THE COUPLE

1. Which method for negotiation appealed the most to each of you?
2. Which were you able to use?
3. Can you think of other issues it might be good to use any of these methods with?

NEGOTIATING IMPASSES

When you come to loggerheads, sometimes it seems as though there is no solution. Try one of these four methods for negotiating differences or impasses. Try them in the spirit of experimentation. They may not solve the problem (or they might), but they might get you unstuck from your impasse.

1. Take turns doing it one partner's way and then the other's for an agreed upon period of time. For example, one person wants to buy takeout on his or her night to cook and the other would rather have a homecooked meal. For one month, try takeout food. For the next month, try homecooked meals. Check in with your partner after two months and discuss the results of the experiment.

2. Split the difference. For example, if one of you wants to go out to eat every weekend and your partner wants to go out only once per month, go out twice per month. If one of you wants to ground your teenager for a month for coming home late and the other thinks it should be for one night, try grounding your child for a week or every weekend for a month.

3. Find another action that would represent a show of good faith to your partner rather than the one he or she is demanding. For example, if your partner wants you to take dancing lessons and you are unwilling, your partner may conclude that you are unwilling to try anything new. Find some other activity besides dancing that he or she would also like to do that you would agree to do that would show your partner that you are willing to try something new.

4. Drop the issue for a time and focus on areas in which both of you can agree and are willing to change. Agree that you will take up this tough issue again, say in a month or six months, but for now, let it go. Time sometimes brings new perspectives or new circumstances that allow for a solution.

Choreograph an Argument

GOALS OF THE EXERCISE

1. To encourage the client to slow down and think.
2. To suggest specific changes to help in discussing differences.

TYPES OF PROBLEMS THIS EXERCISE MAY BE MOST USEFUL FOR

- Anger
- Anxiety
- Blame
- Communication
- Dependency
- Jealousy

SUGGESTIONS FOR PROCESSING THIS EXERCISE WITH THE COUPLE

1. What helped?
2. What did you find outside these suggestions on the assignment sheet that helped?
3. What was difficult and how did you deal with it?

CHOREOGRAPH AN ARGUMENT

> *Emotional people trying to get their way often are the basis of arguments. This exercise provides a framework for keeping the discussion focused on the behaviors you want to change.*

1. Stop and think.

   Exactly what happened that you don't like? Put it in terms of "who did what." Avoid blaming, labeling, or analyzing. Write it below in item #3.

   _____

   Do you need to talk about it or is it something that can be overlooked?

   _____

   _____

   _____

   Is it something that the other person can do something about?

   _____

   What do you want? Write what you are asking for in item 4. Make it crystal clear.

   _____

2. Find a time and place to talk when you can both give your full attention to the issue.

   _____

3. Present the complaint.

   _____

   _____

4. Present one or more suggestions or requests.

_____

_____

_____

_____

5. Negotiate. Before you start negotiating:

- Remember that you are creating a solution that everyone can accept

- Keep looking for a solution to the original problem

- Remember you can take a time out

- Listen and be sure that you understand before you prepare a response

- Do not give in just to end the argument

- Be sure you can and will do what you agree to

- Hold firmly to your values while remaining flexible on how you exemplify them

Is the other person willing and able to do what was requested?

_____

If not, brainstorm possible solutions. Without censoring them, write as many ideas for solutions that you can come up with.

_____

_____

Continue to negotiate for as long as it takes to come up with a solution acceptable to all concerned. Take breaks or days off as necessary. Keep the discussion focused on behavior that will solve the problem.

_____

_____

6. What specific action will be taken? When? By whom?

_____

_____

_____

_____

_____

7. When will you review your progress?

_____

_____

_____

_____

_____

_____

8. The complainant will be looking for any sign of progress or effort that the other person makes regarding the problem. Specifically, watch for the times that they do what they have agreed to do. Write the dates and times below. At the time of the action, acknowledge the behavior to the person making the effort.

_____

_____

_____

_____

_____

_____

_____

Remember to bring completed work sheet to your next appointment.

Go Ape

GOALS OF THE EXERCISE

1. To get couples out of their usual ways of interacting.
2. To access creative and nonverbal ways of communicating and interacting.

TYPES OF PROBLEMS THIS EXERCISE MAY BE MOST USEFUL FOR

- Anger
- Blame
- Communication
- Dependency
- Jealousy
- Midlife Crisis
- Sexual Dysfunction
- Work/Home Role Strain

SUGGESTIONS FOR PROCESSING THIS EXERCISE WITH THE COUPLE

1. How did this exercise feel for each of you?
2. What surprised you the most about this way of arguing?
3. Can you think of other ways that "going ape" might be helpful in your relationship?

GO APE

Unique problems call for unique solutions.

Between now and your next session, whenever you begin to argue, initiate two rules:

1. You may use only those communication methods that apes would have (hugs, grunts, pantomime, etc.).

2. No violence.

When you are finished, answer the following questions:

What was hard about this exercise?

_____

_____

_____

Explain three ways this argument is different from those you have had in the past.

_____

_____

_____

What are three things about arguing this way that are better the way you have been doing it?

_____

_____

_____

List three things you learned from doing this exercise.

_____

_____

_____

How can you use this information in the future?

_____

_____

_____

Remember to bring completed work sheet to your next appointment.

Letter to the Problem

GOALS OF THE EXERCISE

1. To externalize the problem.
2. To join clients.
3. To encourage acceptance and acknowledgment of feelings.

TYPES OF PROBLEMS THIS EXERCISE MAY BE MOST USEFUL FOR

- Alcohol Abuse
- Depression Independent of Relationship Problems
- Depression Due to Relationship
- Eating Disorder
- Personality Differences

SUGGESTIONS FOR PROCESSING THIS EXERCISE WITH THE COUPLE

1. How did this exercise change the way you think about the problem?
2. What did you learn that might be helpful in dealing with the problem?
3. What was it like being the problem?

LETTER TO THE PROBLEM

1. Write a joint letter from the two of you to your problem. You could include:

   • How you see the situation

   • Your feelings about the problem

   • What you want from the problem

   • Consequences of not getting what you want

   • Anything else you like

2. Imagine that you are the problem and write a response to the issues raised in the letter.

3. Write another joint letter to the problem in answer to what the problem has told you.

4. How did your first and second letters to the problem differ?

   _____

   _____

   _____

   _____

5. What did you learn from this exercise?

   _____

   _____

   _____

   _____

Remember to bring completed work sheet to your next appointment.

Going Postal Instead of Going Postal

GOALS OF THE EXERCISE

1. To suggest a safe way to express feelings.
2. To acknowledge each partner's right to his or her feelings.

TYPES OF PROBLEMS THIS EXERCISE MAY BE MOST USEFUL FOR

- Anger
- Blame
- Communication
- Intolerance
- Jealousy
- Loss of Love/Affection

SUGGESTIONS FOR PROCESSING THIS EXERCISE WITH THE COUPLE

1. Allow each partner to discuss the contents of the letter to the extent that he or she thinks it is helpful.
2. What do you want to do with the letter?
3. Will this be the last such letter you will write?

GOING POSTAL INSTEAD OF GOING POSTAL

> *Sometimes we don't resolve an issue at the time that it arises. It might be something from childhood or from an earlier relationship. Frequently, such an issue can be satisfactorily reopened and resolved. This exercise presents one way to do that.*

Write a letter to a person with whom you feel you have unfinished business. Use this sheet to get your thoughts together, then write the letter.

- Write a factual account of the situation that caused the problem.

  _____

  _____

- What haven't you said?

  _____

  _____

- Explain your feelings about the problem.

  _____

  _____

- What do you appreciate about what happened?

  _____

  _____

- What do you not appreciate about what happened?

  _____

  _____

• List any regrets you have about the situation.

_____

_____

• Spell out clearly any wishes, demands, or requests you want to make.

_____

_____

• Is there anything else you want to include in the letter?

_____

_____

After you have composed the letter, answer the following questions:

• What do you want to do with the letter?

_____

_____

• If it can't be delivered or if it is better for you not to do so, list three things that you could do with the letter that might be meaningful to you?

_____

_____

Remember to bring completed work sheet to your next appointment.

Lighten Your Load

GOALS OF THE EXERCISE

1. To physically represent some unfinished emotion or situation for one or both of the partners.
2. To help clients to let go of or finish unfinished business.

TYPES OF PROBLEMS THIS EXERCISE MAY BE MOST USEFUL FOR

- Infidelity
- Jealousy
- Loss of Love/Affection
- Sexual Dysfunction

SUGGESTIONS FOR PROCESSING THIS EXERCISE WITH THE COUPLE

1. How did this exercise affect your feelings about the unfinished or problem situation?
2. Are there any other issues that you think it would be helpful to use this exercise with?
3. How was it not to talk about the problem with your partner?

LIGHTEN YOUR LOAD

> *Sometimes we dwell on problems that can't be easily resolved or perhaps will never be resolved. If you are dwelling on a problem as an individual or as a couple, here's an idea for getting the problem out of your mind.*

Write down the name of the person, the emotion, or the unresolved situation on a piece of paper. Carry it around with you (or both of you carry a copy) for as long as you need to feel as if the paper is now connected to the problem or unfinished business. Then decide on your own or talk over as a couple a place you might leave the piece of paper in order to symbolically leave the problem behind. It might be under a rock, it might be at someone's grave, it might be flushed down the toilet, or thrown into the ocean. Choose a special time (an anniversary of some event, a birthday, or a holiday, such as Independence Day) to get rid of your piece of paper. Make a note on your calendar to have a conversation one month after you do this.

Don't mention the problem to your partner for one month. At that time, sit down and write three things that have changed for each of you since you got rid of the paper.

_____

_____

_____

_____

_____

_____

_____

Remember to bring completed work sheet to your next appointment.

Can Do!

GOALS OF THE EXERCISE

1. To interrupt the usual pattern of conflict between the couple.
2. To externalize the problems and help each partner let some issues go.

TYPES OF PROBLEMS THIS EXERCISE MAY BE MOST USEFUL FOR

- Anger
- Blame
- Communication
- Financial Conflict
- Job Stress
- Work/Home Role Strain

SUGGESTIONS FOR PROCESSING THIS EXERCISE WITH THE COUPLE

1. How did you let go of the problems you did?
2. What did you learn from doing this exercise?
3. How did it feel to delay when you usually deal with things much more quickly?

CAN DO!

We all know that we can't change the past. In spite of that, it's common for people to bring up old problems while trying to solve new ones. This can be destructive and frustrating. Whenever you find yourself revisiting an old injustice, write it on a piece of paper and put it in a can on the top shelf of your kitchen cabinet. Once a month, pull out the can and go through the papers. Decide which memories you want to continue to maintain. Get rid of those that you don't need to hold onto. When you feel the urge to discuss the past, remember that you have it in a can where it won't be forgotten until you are ready to give it your full attention.

How many old problems did you collect?

_____

_____

_____

How many did you discard?

_____

_____

_____

How did you decide which ones to discard?

_____

_____

_____

How did you get rid of them?

_____

_____

_____

Remember to bring completed work sheet to your next appointment.

Plant a Tree

GOALS OF THE EXERCISE

1. To help couples find a physical way of representing some significant experience.
2. To give the message that life is always moving, as is grief, joy, and people's developmental lives.

TYPES OF PROBLEMS THIS EXERCISE MAY BE MOST USEFUL FOR

- Life-Changing Event
- Midlife Crisis

SUGGESTIONS FOR PROCESSING THIS EXERCISE WITH THE COUPLE

1. What was your experience with this exercise?
2. What advice would you now give others who are facing similar issues as you were when you did this exercise?
3. What did you learn about yourself in the choices you made designing this tree-planting ritual?

PLANT A TREE

The old tradition of marking important dates by planting a tree has been largely lost in our urban society. In the past, people planted trees to mark births, deaths, anniversaries, and other important events. You may find it helpful to revive this old tradition and create your own ritual around it. This type of ritual can have unexpected benefits for years as you watch the tree grow.

Take some time to think about the following questions. If appropriate, include friends and family in the planning.

Who do you want to be present?

_____

_____

What kind of tree is most appropriate?

_____

_____

Who will dig the hole and plant the tree?

_____

_____

What would you want said and by whom? You may want to include prayers, poems, or music. Or perhaps silence.

_____

_____

Would you like to put anything in the hole with the tree?

_____

_____

Do you want to include a meal or refreshments? If so, what?

_____

_____

Is there anything else that you would like to include?

_____

_____

Remember to bring completed work sheet to your next appointment.

Section II

General Issues/Values Conflicts for Couples

Value Your Differences

GOALS OF THE EXERCISE

1. To help couples understand their differences.
2. To help couples appreciate their different values.

TYPES OF PROBLEMS THIS EXERCISE MAY BE MOST USEFUL FOR

- Communication
- Life-Changing Events
- Religion/Spirituality Differences

SUGGESTIONS FOR PROCESSING THIS EXERCISE WITH THE COUPLE

1. What surprised you about your partner's values or differences from your ways of thinking about situations?
2. In what areas did you have similar or the same values or perceptions?
3. How will doing this exercise help you in the future?

VALUE YOUR DIFFERENCES

> *It's easy to say that having different kinds of people in the world keeps things from getting boring and quite another thing to live with some of those people. Learning to value differences in others is a challenge for most of us at one time or another. Often we assume that everyone, especially our partners, have the same values, motivations, and ways of understanding the world that we do. If they act in a way that upsets us or perplexes us, usually that indicates that they have a different understanding or different value from ours. There are several ways to value those differences rather than have them be sources of conflict or hurt. The first is to be genuinely curious about how the other person makes sense of what they did.*

Each day for the next week, note a way that your partner is different from you or acts differently than you would. Ask them to explain how they understood the situation. Do not criticize or judge them or their explanation. Just try to put yourself in their shoes and understand how they could see things in that light or with those values.

_____

_____

_____

Explain to your partner how you understood or thought about that same situation differently. Again, do not try to convince them that your way is right and theirs is wrong. Just communicate your way of making sense of the situation.

_____

_____

_____

For each difference, note at least one way or context in which your partner's viewpoint or behavior could be valuable.

_____

_____

Remember to bring completed work sheet to your next appointment.

Accountability

GOALS OF THE EXERCISE

1. To help couples recognize places where they have been non-accountable.
2. To help couples develop accountability.

TYPES OF PROBLEMS THIS EXERCISE MAY BE MOST USEFUL FOR

- Blame
- Depression Due to Relationship Problems
- Financial Conflict
- Infidelity
- Jealousy
- Physical Abuse
- Psychological Abuse
- Sexual Abuse

SUGGESTIONS FOR PROCESSING THIS EXERCISE WITH THE COUPLE

1. Where did you find holes in your accountability?
2. How did you talk about the situation differently when you spoke about it in an accountable way?
3. How will doing this exercise change your relationship in the future?

ACCOUNTABILITY

> *Accountability has two components: (1) Acknowledging what you did or do and (2) not giving excuses or explanations to suggest you couldn't help doing what you did.*

Sometimes arguments or conflicts arise when one or both of you are not being accountable for something you do or have done. Instead of being accountable, you give excuses or reasons why you couldn't help doing what you did.

Typical excuses or explanations:

Genetic: I've just got this biological/genetic/biochemical nature or condition that makes me act this way.

Developmental: I was raised this way and therefore I have to act this way.

Interpersonal: He made me do it. It was a reaction. If she didn't nag me I wouldn't have hit her.

In this exercise, discuss some behavior that upset your partner and for which you haven't been accountable. Try to reflect an acknowledgment of accountability. Just describe what behavior you did without offering any rationalization or excuse.

_____

_____

_____

_____

_____

_____

_____

Remember to bring completed work sheet to your next appointment.

Restoring Trust and Faith When One Partner Has Betrayed the Relationship

GOALS OF THE EXERCISE

1. To help repair betrayed trust.
2. To call the partner who betrayed trust to accountability.

TYPES OF PROBLEMS THIS EXERCISE MAY BE MOST USEFUL FOR

- Infidelity
- Jealousy
- Physical Abuse
- Psychological Abuse
- Sexual Abuse

SUGGESTIONS FOR PROCESSING THIS EXERCISE WITH THE COUPLE

1. [To the partner who betrayed] How was it to acknowledge and take responsibility for your actions?
2. [To the partner who was betrayed] How was it to hear your partner acknowledge and take responsibility for the betrayal?
3. How will doing this exercise affect the future of your relationship?

RESTORING TRUST AND FAITH WHEN ONE PARTNER HAS BETRAYED THE RELATIONSHIP

If one of you has violated the boundaries or integrity of the relationship by doing something unethical or harmful (like lying, being unfaithful, spending money you had agreed not to spend, keeping a secret that affected your partner in a negative way, telling a secret that embarrassed or betrayed your partner, etc.), there are steps you could take to restore trust and integrity to your relationship.

1. Acknowledge that you messed up. You could do this in writing or face-to-face. Make sure in your acknowledgment that you don't offer excuses or reasons that let you off the hook in terms of responsibility. Just describe what you did. The discussion of reasons and extenuating circumstances is usually best left for another time. Write out the facts of the situation that you need to convey.

2. Make a promise that you won't betray your partner in that way in the future and follow through with actions that say you mean what you say. Be scrupulous about your future behavior in the area in which you messed up. Don't allow yourself to be sidetracked if your partner expresses skepticism. Detail the promises that you want to make.

3. Offer an apology and ask you partner if there is anything you could do to rectify things. If possible, make amends in the way they request. Note anything that your partner tells you that you can do. Immediately write your plan to be sure that you get the job done.

Inequities

GOALS OF THE EXERCISE

1. To help couples more equitably divide household chores.
2. To raise awareness of inequities in the relationship.

TYPES OF PROBLEMS THIS EXERCISE MAY BE MOST USEFUL FOR

- Job Stress
- Work/Home Role Strain

SUGGESTIONS FOR PROCESSING THIS EXERCISE WITH THE COUPLE

1. Were you surprised by the division of the tasks?
2. What did you learn from doing this exercise?
3. How do you think that the ideas you got from your family of origin and your culture influence how you divide tasks?

INEQUITIES

Having the sense that one is being treated unfairly can be toxic to a relationship. Chores and household responsibilities can be a source of feelings of inequity in a relationship. This exercise can assist in equally distributing household chores. The principle can also be applied to other situations where fairness is an issue.

List all the chores you want to divide:

_____

_____

_____

_____

_____

_____

_____

_____

_____

_____

_____

First divide up whatever tasks you can agree about. Divide the remaining chores into two groups. Let one person divide the chores and the other person will choose which group they will do. If you can't decide which person will do the dividing, flip a coin. List the chores and who will do them

_____

_____

_____

_____

_____

_____

_____

_____

_____

_____

_____

_____

Set a date when you will meet again. If you are dissatisfied with the current division of labor, change roles in this division process.

_____

_____

_____

_____

_____

_____

_____

_____

_____

_____

_____

_____

_____

Remember to bring completed work sheet to your next appointment.

Feeling Responsible: Who Initiates Things That Need to Be Done

GOALS OF THE EXERCISE

1. To help the couple become aware of inequities in who takes responsibility for and initiates joint tasks.
2. To introduce an awareness and discussion of gender training influences on each partner and the relationship.

TYPES OF PROBLEMS THIS EXERCISE MAY BE MOST USEFUL FOR

- Financial Conflict
- Job Stress
- Parenting Conflict
- Work/Home Role Strain

SUGGESTIONS FOR PROCESSING THIS EXERCISE WITH THE COUPLE

1. Were you aware of this issue before you did this exercise?
2. What ways were you trained as a man or as a woman in the areas of responsibility?
3. Do you agree with this societal programming or are there places where it doesn't fit for you and your relationship?
4. How might you challenge this inequity in feeling responsible?

FEELING RESPONSIBLE: WHO INITIATES THINGS THAT NEED TO BE DONE

> *Sometimes chores and family and household tasks are divided somewhat equitably, but one person still feels as if he or she (usually she, since we train women in this culture to take responsibility for relationships and other people, as well as household chores) has the burden for making things happen. This may be an issue in your relationship.*

Sit down and make a list all the chores and family and household responsibilities you have as a couple. To help you think about this issue of responsibility, here is a list that you can use to clarify who usually initiates, does, or feels responsible for each item:

- Cleaning the house
- Doing the cooking
- Grocery shopping
- Cleaning up after a meal
- Doing the laundry
- Making doctor's or dentist's appointments for self or others
- Making appointments for getting the car serviced or repaired
- Calling household repair people
- Meeting household repair people when they arrive to do their work
- Noticing that things around the house need repair or servicing
- Compiling the information for tax preparation
- Paying the bills
- Making a budget
- Making money
- Coordinating children's school and after-school activities
- Caring for the children
- Arranging for childcare when neither parent is available

- Making social arrangements
- Driving or arranging transportation for children to activities, school or friends
- Arranging or planning vacations
- Doing yardwork
- Calling friends or relatives to stay in touch
- Writing friends or relatives to stay in touch
- Buying Christmas, Hanukkah, Kwanzaa, birthday, or other special occasion cards
- Shopping for clothing
- Maintaining clothing (doing laundry, dropping off/picking up dry cleaning, ironing, replacing buttons, mending, etc.)
- Helping children with homework
- Writing or sending special occasion cards

_____

_____

_____

_____

_____

Is there an imbalance in who usually takes responsibility for these tasks? If so, have the partner who usually takes less responsibility agree to take on three of the tasks the other partner usually takes responsibility for during the next month. List those three tasks:

_____

_____

_____

At the end of the month, sit down and discuss what each of you have learned and make plans to change anything about the responsibilities that seems appropriate at that time.

Remember to bring completed work sheet to your next appointment.

Intimacy

GOALS OF THE EXERCISE

1. To help couples discover the things that enhance their feelings of closeness.
2. To help couples increase the actions that enhance intimacy.

TYPES OF PROBLEMS THIS EXERCISE MAY BE MOST USEFUL FOR

- Communication
- Infidelity
- Jealousy
- Sexual Dysfunction

SUGGESTIONS FOR PROCESSING THIS EXERCISE WITH THE COUPLE

1. What things helped each of you feel closer to your partner?
2. What makes those things more likely to occur?
3. What changes do you plan to make now that you have noticed these things about the intimacy in your relationship?

INTIMACY

Intimacy is one of those things that's hard to define but you know when it's there. It's hard to make yourself feel more intimate, but sometimes you can do things that will make you feel closer. If you are looking to increase your intimacy, you might find it helpful to track your feelings of intimacy and see what is different when you feel closer to your partner, then make those things happen more often.

Below is a graph. Imagine your intimacy on a scale of 0 to 10, with 0 being before you knew each other and 10 being the closest you've ever felt. Each day between now and your next session, plot your feeling of intimacy from 1 to 10. On the back of this sheet, note what helped you feel closer that day, or at least what helped you feel as close as you did.

Remember to bring completed work sheet to your next appointment.

103

Styles of and
Motivation for Arguing

GOALS OF THE EXERCISE

1. To encourage the couple to slow down and think.
2. To suggest specific changes to help in discussing differences.

TYPES OF PROBLEMS THIS EXERCISE MAY
BE MOST USEFUL FOR

- Anger
- Blame
- Communication
- Personality Differences

SUGGESTIONS FOR PROCESSING THIS
EXERCISE WITH THE COUPLE

1. What helped?
2. What did you find outside these suggestions on the assignment sheet that helped?
3. What was difficult and how did you deal with it?

STYLES OF AND MOTIVATION FOR ARGUING

Just about anything can become a habit and that includes arguing. One of the best ways to break a habit is to make it impossible to perform. You can do that by continuing what you do, but changing a detail that makes it a slightly different behavior from what you did in the past. This is an exercise in changing your style of arguing. It may give you ideas about other things you can change as well.

Between now and your next session, be alert to the subtle beginnings of an argument. At the first hint or suspicion of an impending argument, remind your partner that this is an opportunity to work on changing your old habits. The person who first suspects that the argument is starting goes first. Go to separate rooms. Write whatever it is that you want to say. When finished, give the paper to your partner, who then has the opportunity to read it and respond on paper. Repeat this process as long as you think it is helpful. Then answer the following questions:

1. How did the course of the argument differ from your usual disagreements?

   _____

   _____

2. What was better about doing it this way?

   _____

   _____

3. What were the disadvantages?

   _____

   _____

4. What can you take from this experience and apply to your disagreements in the future?

   _____

   _____

Remember to bring completed work sheet to your next appointment.

Forgiveness

GOALS OF THE EXERCISE

1. To move clients closer to forgiveness about something that they have been holding feelings of resentment and a desire for vengeance.
2. To help clients recognize the price they pay for anger and resentment.
3. To challenge the client to either get satisfaction from the other person or let go of the urge to get even.

TYPES OF PROBLEMS THIS EXERCISE MAY BE MOST USEFUL FOR

- Anger
- Communication
- Infidelity
- Jealousy
- Physical Abuse
- Sexual Abuse

SUGGESTIONS FOR PROCESSING THIS EXERCISE WITH THE COUPLE

1. What do you feel you are owed?
2. What are the advantages and disadvantages of remaining angry?
3. Have you let the other person know what you want?
4. How will you know that you have forgiven them?

FORGIVENESS

While it is common for people to hold a grudge when they have been wronged, there is a growing body of evidence that suggests that unresolved anger is bad for your physical and mental health. While it may be impossible and even undesirable to forget what happened, it is surprising what some people can forgive. What is forgiveness? A popular definition holds that when you forgive, you simply write off any debt that you feel is owed to you. In other words, it is a decision.

1. What do you rightfully deserve that would even the score?

_____

_____

_____

2. What price do you pay for holding on to this debt?

_____

_____

_____

3. Have you let the other person know what you think you deserve?

_____

_____

_____

4. If not, would you?

_____

_____

_____

5. Can they or are they willing to give you what you want?

_____

_____

_____

6. How would you be better off if you gave up on getting even?

_____

_____

_____

7. How long are you willing to hold on to your anger?

_____

_____

_____

Remember to bring completed work sheet to your next appointment.

Money/Financial Conflicts

GOALS OF THE EXERCISE

1. To help the couple get a clear idea of how their money is used.
2. To encourage the couple to make conscious decisions after discussion about where to spend their money.

TYPES OF PROBLEMS THIS EXERCISE MAY BE MOST USEFUL FOR

- Financial Conflict
- Job Stress
- Work/Home Role Strain

SUGGESTIONS FOR PROCESSING THIS EXERCISE WITH THE COUPLE

1. In what categories did you spend the most money?
2. In what categories did you spend the least money?
3. What surprised you?
4. What do you like about how you spent your money?
5. How do you want to change?
6. What will be difficult about changing?

MONEY/FINANCIAL CONFLICTS

> *Money serves a wide variety of purposes for people. If you are going to control your finances, it will help to know where your money goes and what need it is filling for you. There is an old saying, "If you don't know where you are, it's hard to get where you're going." This exercise is a good way to find out where you are in regard to money and begin thinking about your relationship and priorities with money.*

Keep track of where you spend every penny for one month (especially cash). You may need to carry a little notebook with you at all times to record the data. Enter the totals below, adding as many additional categories as you need. Avoid creating a miscellaneous category; be specific.

ATM fees

Auto

Cable

Charity

Childcare

Cigarettes

Cleaning supplies

Clothing

Credit card interest

Dental

Diapers

Eating out

Entertainment

Gifts

Groceries

Hobbies

Housing

Insurance

Liquor

Medical

Telephone

Toiletries

Transportation

Utilities

As you look over the totals, what surprises you?

_____

_____

During this month, how much did you save?

_____

_____

What are five things that you use money for?

_____

_____

_____

_____

_____

Would you like to change any of those?

_____

_____

_____

Remember to bring completed work sheet to your next appointment.

A Common Destination

GOALS OF THE EXERCISE

1. To help the couple get a clear idea of their vacation preferences.
2. To help the couple find and plan a mutually agreeable vacation.
3. To help the couple develop new problem-solving skills.

TYPES OF PROBLEMS THIS EXERCISE MAY BE MOST USEFUL FOR

- Communication
- Recreational Activities Dispute

SUGGESTIONS FOR PROCESSING THIS EXERCISE WITH THE COUPLE

1. In what categories did you agree the most?
2. Did you clarify anything for yourself about your vacation preferences?
3. What surprised you about your partner's lists?
4. Based on this exercise, could you now make a mutually agreeable vacation plan for your next vacation?
5. If not, could you agree to let each partner plan every other vacation, taking into account the other partner's preferences?

A COMMON DESTINATION

> *Vacation is supposed to be a time of rest and relaxation, however, sometimes couples disagree on their preferred styles of vacation or destination. This exercise may help resolve conflicts about vacations.*

1. Each of you list your ideal vacation, including: ideal locations; ideal activities during vacation; friends you wouldn't mind or would like to have along with you:

   _____

   _____

   Ideal length of vacation:

   _____

   Ideal frequency of vacation:

   _____

   Ideal time of the year for vacation:

   _____

   Ideal amount of money or limit for expenditures for vacation:

   _____

2. Compare notes with your partner. Don't judge or make fun of your partner's preferences. List on a separate sheet any common areas of agreement on your list.

3. Find three vacations that fulfill as many of your common preferences as possible and write them below.

   _____

   _____

   _____

Remember to bring completed work sheet to your next appointment.

Negotiating Socializing Preference Differences

GOALS OF THE EXERCISE

1. To help the couple get a clear idea of their socializing preferences.
2. To help the couple find and plan mutually agreeable social arrangements.

TYPES OF PROBLEMS THIS EXERCISE MAY BE MOST USEFUL FOR

- Blended-Family Problems
- Communication
- Job Stress
- Recreational Activities Dispute
- Work/Home Role Strain

SUGGESTIONS FOR PROCESSING THIS EXERCISE WITH THE COUPLE

1. In what categories did you agree the most?
2. Did you clarify anything for yourself about your preferences?
3. What surprised you about your partner's lists?
4. Based on this exercise, could you now make mutually agreeable social plans?

NEGOTIATING SOCIALIZING PREFERENCE DIFFERENCES

> *Sometimes couples disagree about how they want to spend their social time or how much they want to interact with each other or others outside of their relationship. At one time, the big complaint was spending time with the in-laws. Now, dual careers, the Internet, computer games, fax machines, and the proliferation of television channels and videos provide many areas of potential conflict and distraction. This exercise may help clarify and resolve conflicts about these areas.*

1. Each of you make a list of how you like to spend your social time.

Individual time: _____

How much? _____

Doing what? _____

Time with your partner: _____

How much? _____

Doing what? _____

Time with friends: _____

How much? _____

Doing what? _____

Time with other family members: _____

Children: _____

How much? _____

Doing what? _____

In-laws: _____

How much? _____

Doing what? _____

Extended family: _____

How much? _____

Doing what? _____

Hobbies: _____

How much? _____

Doing what? _____

Together or alone? _____

Entertainment: _____

How much? _____

Doing what? _____

Together or alone? _____

2. Compare notes with your partner. Don't judge or make fun of your partner's preferences. List on a separate sheet any common areas of agreement on your list.

3. Negotiate, perhaps with the help of your counselor, areas of disagreement.

Remember to bring completed work sheet to your next appointment.

Section III

Specific Problem Areas for Couples

Chronic or Unproductive Arguments

GOALS OF THE EXERCISE

1. To help couples interrupt and change unproductive conflict patterns and habits.
2. To help each partner find new ways of accomplishing their goals more effectively.

TYPES OF PROBLEMS THIS EXERCISE MAY BE MOST USEFUL FOR

- Anger
- Blame
- Communication
- Intolerance

SUGGESTIONS FOR PROCESSING THIS EXERCISE WITH THE COUPLE

1. Was there anything on the tape that surprised you?
2. Embarrassed you?
3. What do you plan to change based on this exercise?

CHRONIC OR UNPRODUCTIVE ARGUMENTS

Some arguments seem to get repeated over and over with nothing getting settled. Sometimes this happens because we are so involved in the argument that we don't stop to listen to ourselves. This assignment is designed to help you do that and to see what a difference that can make.

Tape record one of your arguments. Do this only with the full knowledge and consent of both persons. Later, find a calm time to review the argument. Before you listen to the tape, write as clearly as possible what you were trying to accomplish. In this step, be careful to define what you were trying to resolve (for example, "Deciding how to manage our money in a responsible way.") and not the solution you were suggesting (for example, "Getting him or her to stop spending so much money on clothes.").

_____

_____

_____

_____

Now, review the tape, stopping it every three minutes or less. Note everything that either of you does that moves you even a little bit toward your goal, as you stated above. For the purposes of this exercise, do your best to ignore the things that don't move the two of you toward your goal.

_____

_____

_____

_____

When you are finished:

What did you learn from this exercise?

_____

_____

_____

Would it help to do it again? Why or why not?

_____

_____

_____

How can you use this information in future discussions?

_____

_____

_____

Remember to bring completed work sheet to your next appointment.

Verbal Abuse

GOALS OF THE EXERCISE

1. To help couples recognize and identify verbal abuse.
2. To help the partner who feels verbally abused escape from some of the damage to his or her confidence or self-esteem.

TYPES OF PROBLEMS THIS EXERCISE MAY BE MOST USEFUL FOR

- Anger
- Blame
- Communication
- Psychological Abuse

SUGGESTIONS FOR PROCESSING THIS EXERCISE WITH THE COUPLE

1. Did this exercise help either of you make any changes?
2. Did it help you recognize or learn anything new?
3. What kinds of things did you write on your lists?

VERBAL ABUSE

Verbal abuse is an attempt to control or manipulate someone by using words or speaking in a manner that demeans them. If you live with a person who verbally abuses you, it can be very difficult to keep a realistic image of yourself. Here are some suggestions that may help.

By identifying verbal abuse, you can remind yourself that you needn't accept it. Remember that verbal abuse is about control and manipulation. Write below some of the abusive words or expressions that your partner uses.

_____

_____

_____

List names and phone numbers of people you know and trust to have objective opinions of you.

_____

_____

_____

Look up and write down the phone number(s) of your local abuse prevention service(s). Use them if you need them.

_____

_____

_____

_____

Write three messages of self-affirmation or encouragement that you know to be true about yourself but sometimes forget after you've been attacked.

_____

_____

_____

List any inspirational books, pictures, mementos, or other items that you can look at and touch when you need to remind yourself of your self-worth.

_____

_____

_____

Write your reason(s) for staying in this abusive situation and review them from time to time to see if they still make sense to you.

_____

_____

_____

Keep this paper in a safe place so you can find it when you need support.

_____

_____

_____

Remember to bring completed work sheet to your next appointment.

Boxing Clutter to a TKO

GOALS OF THE EXERCISE

1. To help couples find a resolution to conflicts about clutter and procrastination.
2. To help the procrastinating partner get moving to clean up the clutter.
3. To empower the other partner.

TYPES OF PROBLEMS THIS EXERCISE MAY BE MOST USEFUL FOR

- Life-Changing Events
- Work/Home Role Strain

SUGGESTIONS FOR PROCESSING THIS EXERCISE WITH THE COUPLE

1. How did it feel to put the date or have the date put on the box?
2. Does this exercise feel as if it will be helpful in resolving your conflicts about clutter and procrastination?
3. What do you fear will happen in a year? What do you hope will happen in a year?

BOXING CLUTTER TO A TKO

> *If one of you keeps old mail, papers, articles, magazines, and other things that clutter the house, but could be gone through, organized, and thrown out or filed and it drives the other partner crazy, you might try this idea.*

The partner who is most bothered by the clutter can gather up the mess and place it into a box. The box is labeled with a date one year from the day it is placed in the box. The box can be stored in a closet or garage or left out in the open. By the date on the box, the other partner must either have gone through and organized and cleaned out the box or the other partner has permission to throw the box out.

Use the rest of this page to make notes about anything you want to remember to discuss with your therapist in your next session.

_____

_____

_____

_____

_____

_____

_____

_____

_____

Remember to bring completed work sheet to your next appointment.

Separating Work from Home Life

GOALS OF THE EXERCISE

1. To help the couple clarify areas in which work impinges on home life in an unhelpful way.
2. To help the couple make changes to separate home from work.

TYPES OF PROBLEMS THIS EXERCISE MAY BE MOST USEFUL FOR

- Anxiety
- Depression Independent of Relationship Problems
- Financial Conflict
- Job Stress
- Work/Home Role Strain

SUGGESTIONS FOR PROCESSING THIS EXERCISE WITH THE COUPLE

1. In which areas are the most crucial in making the separation of work from home?
2. Which areas did you both agree that work is impinging unhelpfully on home life?
3. What was the agreement you made?

SEPARATING WORK FROM HOME LIFE

If you have a conflict around separating your home life from one or both of your work lives, use this exercise to clarify and negotiate a good separation of one from the other.

1. List the ways that one or both of you think that work life impinges on your home life, your relationship, or your family life and time. Examine these areas:

   • Working late

   • Computer use

   • Time at work versus time at home, with family, friends, or spouse

   • Space (work taking over areas at home)

   • People (work relationships impinging on home)

   • Phone calls (at home from work or from home to work)

2. Have a discussion about changes that each and both of you would like in any of these areas.

   _____

   _____

   _____

3. Make an agreement for either or both of you to make at least three changes over the next six months.

   _____

   _____

   _____

Remember to bring completed work sheet to your next appointment.

Planned Spontaneity

GOALS OF THE EXERCISE

1. To revitalize couples' romantic life.
2. To help people learn how to be more romantic from their past, from books, and from others.

TYPES OF PROBLEMS THIS EXERCISE MAY BE MOST USEFUL FOR

- Anxiety
- Depression Due to Relationship Problems
- Infidelity
- Jealousy
- Loss of Love/Affection
- Sexual Dysfunction

SUGGESTIONS FOR PROCESSING THIS EXERCISE WITH THE COUPLE

1. Did you feel more loving as you did more romantic things?
2. Did your partner seem more loving to you after you did some more romantic things?
3. How could you use what you learned from doing this exercise in your future relationship?

PLANNED SPONTANEITY

> *It takes ongoing effort to keep a relationship fresh and alive. But what if you're among the ranks of the romantically challenged? For many people, exciting, spontaneous activities are things they observe others doing that make them say, "Why don't I think of doing those things?" One way to answer this query is to plan some spontaneous activities that break your old mold. Remember that many new activities feel awkward and uncomfortable when you are learning them. If you do this exercise frequently enough, you may find that you start to enjoy being romantic.*

1. List ten or more things that you and your partner have done that he or she considered romantic.

2. Go to the library or bookstore and find one of the many popular books that gives ideas for romantic things to do. Find ten or more that you would consider doing and write them below.

_____

_____

_____

_____

_____

_____

_____

_____

3. Over the next month, watch and listen to what goes on around you for things that other people do that are signs of caring. Listen to coworkers. Pay attention to television shows. Use any and all sources of information. Note five things you learn.

_____

_____

_____

_____

4. Once a week get out your list and look it over for inspiration. Plan a specific time to surprise your partner with your activity.

Feel free to add to your list in the future and indicate things that are particularly successful.

Remember to bring completed work sheet to your next appointment.

A Safe Place for the Traumatic Memories

GOALS OF THE EXERCISE

1. To safely contain the trauma of the affair.
2. To get the details of the affair acknowledged in a way that doesn't create so much post-traumatic stress.

TYPES OF PROBLEMS THIS EXERCISE MAY BE MOST USEFUL FOR

- Infidelity
- Jealousy
- Life-Changing Event

SUGGESTIONS FOR PROCESSING THIS EXERCISE WITH THE COUPLE

1. How was it to write or record the details of the affair?
2. How is it to know that those details have been acknowledged?
3. Is it better to have those details locked up for a while?

A SAFE PLACE FOR THE TRAUMATIC MEMORIES

> *Sometimes the person who has been betrayed is obsessed with learning details about the affair. These details can become an obsession that prevents the person who has been betrayed from letting go of the hurt.*

Don't ask your partner for details. You may hear things that will haunt you for years, images that you will find hard to forget or get over. Once you know the broad outlines of what happened, let it rest for awhile. If you find you are still haunted by questions, have your partner write out or record all the details and put the record of the affair in a safety deposit box. Give the key to a friend with instructions not to let you have the key for a year. If you still feel the need to know, look at the material after a year. Most people don't want to see it by then, as they have some distance and don't want to open themselves to the pain again.

Chronic Lateness from Work

GOALS OF THE EXERCISE

1. To help the couple interrupt and change unproductive conflicts about lateness when returning home from work.
2. To create an incentive for the late partner to come home on time.

TYPES OF PROBLEMS THIS EXERCISE MAY BE MOST USEFUL FOR

- Financial Conflict
- Jealousy
- Job Stress
- Work/Home Role Strain

SUGGESTIONS FOR PROCESSING THIS EXERCISE WITH THE COUPLE

1. What changed as a result of this exercise?
2. Did your partner come home any earlier?
3. What kinds of effort did it take to get home on time?
4. Did you get more time to do what you wanted as a couple and was it worth it?

CHRONIC LATENESS FROM WORK

> *If you are constantly arguing about one partner being home late from work, try this exercise. Stop hassling the partner who is late. Stop complaining ineffectively. For every minute the partner is late (agree on a time that both of you think is reasonable and gives the person who is late some leeway), the other partner gets to redeem them at the end of the week for that same amount of minutes doing anything as a couple that he or she would like to do.*

Write the target time here: _____

Record the following information:

Day 1

Time arrived: _____

Target time: _____

Difference, if actual time is later than target time: _____

If you arrived on time, how did you make that happen?

_____

Day 2

Time arrived: _____

Target time: _____

Difference, if actual time is later than target time: _____

If you arrived on time, how did you make that happen?

_____

Day 3

Time arrived: _____

Target time: _____

Difference, if actual time is later than target time: _____

If you arrived on time, how did you make that happen?

_____

Day 4

Time arrived: _____

Target time: _____

Difference, if actual time is later than target time: _____

If you arrived on time, how did you make that happen?

_____

Day 5

Time arrived: _____

Target time: _____

Difference, if actual time is later than target time: _____

If you arrived on time, how did you make that happen?

_____

Remember to bring completed work sheet to your next appointment.

How to Support a Partner with a Chronic or Serious Illness

GOALS OF THE EXERCISE

1. To help the couple weather the difficult challenge of chronic illness.
2. To refocus the couples' attention from the problem to the heroic aspects of the illness in their relationship or from the partner with the illness.

TYPES OF PROBLEMS THIS EXERCISE MAY BE MOST USEFUL FOR

- Anxiety
- Communication
- Life-Changing Events

SUGGESTIONS FOR PROCESSING THIS EXERCISE WITH THE COUPLE

1. What surprised you about your partner's list?
2. Did you notice these strengths before? If so, are they more clear to you now?
3. How was it to hear or read the letter your partner wrote?

HOW TO SUPPORT A PARTNER WITH A CHRONIC OR SERIOUS ILLNESS

> *Illness, especially chronic or catastrophic illness, often erodes a person's self-esteem and confidence. It can lead you to focus on all the things you can't do or all the trouble you cause your partner or others. If you are the partner who is not ill, you may not know how to respond to the despondency. It is important to acknowledge the person's feelings and not try to talk them out of those feelings. But in addition, it can important to acknowledge your partner's strengths and capabilities.*

List five ways in which your partner has made impressive efforts to come back from or cope with the illness. Write your partner a letter and give it to him or her or read it aloud letting him or her know you have noticed those efforts and abilities.

_____

_____

_____

_____

_____

List five things that you appreciate about your partner despite or because of the illness.

_____

_____

_____

_____

_____

List five strengths that your partner brings to life and to the experience of illness.

_____

_____

_____

_____

_____

Remember to bring completed work sheet to your next appointment.

Set Limits with Consequences

GOALS OF THE EXERCISE

1. To help one partner draw limits for safety.
2. To help stop violence or dangerous behavior in the relationship.

TYPES OF PROBLEMS THIS EXERCISE MAY BE MOST USEFUL FOR

- Alcohol Abuse
- Anger
- Eating Disorder
- Infidelity
- Jealousy
- Physical Abuse

SUGGESTIONS FOR PROCESSING THIS EXERCISE WITH THE COUPLE

1. Are you ready to have the conversation?
2. Tell me your plan and the words you will use.
3. What will you do if your partner won't cooperate or gets belligerent?

SET LIMITS WITH CONSEQUENCES

> *Sometimes even though you've used all your communications skills, your partner may continue to act abusively or otherwise cause harm to you or someone else. When you reach that realization, you may want to draw the line. You may know that you've reached this point when you are more concerned with protecting yourself or someone else than in changing your partner's behavior. This exercise can help you clarify your thinking in an emotional situation.*

State the behavior that you can no longer tolerate.

_____

_____

_____

What are the limits of what you are willing to tolerate. Be as specific as possible.

_____

_____

_____

What consequences are you willing to set if the limits are crossed? Be absolutely certain that the consequence is something under your control and that you are willing to act on it.

_____

_____

_____

Think about how you will present this to your partner so that it is most likely to be taken seriously and to be seen not so much as an ultimatum as something you are doing to take care of personal needs that you deserve to have met.

_____

_____

_____

Where and when will you have your conversation?

_____

_____

_____

What words will you use?

_____

_____

_____

Do you need to take any measures for your safety?

_____

_____

_____

Remember to bring completed work sheet to your next appointment.

Sexual Issues and Problems

Mix 'N' Match Sexual Menu for Expanding Your Sex Life

GOALS OF THE EXERCISE

1. To help couples communicate their sexual interests to each other.
2. To help couples revitalize their sexual relationship.

TYPES OF PROBLEMS THIS EXERCISE MAY BE MOST USEFUL FOR

- Communication
- Jealousy
- Loss of Love/Affection
- Sexual Dysfunction

SUGGESTIONS FOR PROCESSING THIS EXERCISE WITH THE COUPLE

1. Did doing this exercise result in any changes in your sex life?
2. What surprised you most about your own preferences? Your partner's?
3. Do you think this is a helpful exercise for you as a couple and that you would do it again sometime in the future?

MIX 'N' MATCH SEXUAL MENU FOR EXPANDING YOUR SEX LIFE

Many couples grow stale in their sexual life, in part because they fall into routines and in part because they don't tell each other new sexual things they might like to try. Others find that their preferences change and if they never talk about it, they don't get satisfied and lose interest. This exercise can help restore new creativity and excitement to your sex life.

These two columns represent the parts of our bodies that are capable of providing stimulation to others (The Doers) and those parts of our bodies that are capable of experiencing stimulation or pleasure (The Doees). Add your own body parts to the list if there are any missing. Your task is to draw a line between each of these columns to indicate which might be interesting for you to explore or activities that you really enjoy. After you connect the columns with lines, discuss your choices with your partner. You may want to do the chart together, but if you do it alone, show your chart to your partner and talk about it. You may want to exchange lists and keep them for future reference.

The Doers	**The Doees**
Fingers	Mouth
Tongue	Penis
Penis	Vagina
Vagina	Breasts
Mouth	Nipples
Hand	Anus
Skin	Clitoris
	Skin

Feel free to add in the remaining space anything that you would like your partner to know about what gives you pleasure.

_____

_____

Remember to bring completed work sheet to your next appointment.

Pleasure Teaching Session

GOALS OF THE EXERCISE

1. To facilitate couples learning about each others' sexual preferences.
2. To revitalize the couple's sexual life.

TYPES OF PROBLEMS THIS EXERCISE MAY BE MOST USEFUL FOR

- Communication
- Jealousy
- Loss of Love/Affection
- Sexual Dysfunction

SUGGESTIONS FOR PROCESSING THIS EXERCISE WITH THE COUPLE

1. Which role was easier for you? What does this say about you?
2. What was most difficult about this exercise for you?
3. What were three things you learned?
4. What does it say about you as a couple that you carried out this assignment?

PLEASURE TEACHING SESSION

Pick a time when you both have nothing pressing or scheduled. Reserve several hours and find a private place. You may have to rent a hotel room if you have children at home. Choose which person is to be the teacher and which the student. The student's task is to learn from the teacher what gives the teacher pleasure. The teacher may use words, sounds, pictures, or guided movements to indicate what feels good (and, of course, what doesn't feel good). The teacher must be sure to bring whatever materials are necessary to enhance his or her pleasure (special clothes or outfits, sexual toys, massage oil, condoms, books, videotapes, etc.). The student may also bring items he or she thinks would bring pleasure, but only introduce them with the teacher's permission. On another occasion, switch roles, with the student becoming the teacher.

Dealing with Impotence

GOALS OF THE EXERCISE

1. To facilitate couples working together to resolve impotence.
2. To take the pressure off the male to "perform" sexually.

TYPES OF PROBLEMS THIS EXERCISE MAY BE MOST USEFUL FOR

- Communication
- Jealousy
- Loss of Love/Affection
- Life-Changing Events
- Sexual Dysfunction

SUGGESTIONS FOR PROCESSING THIS EXERCISE WITH THE COUPLE

1. What did you learn from this exercise?
2. Did the man have a stronger and longer lasting erection doing this exercise?
3. What did you talk about during the discussion part of the exercise?

DEALING WITH IMPOTENCE

Part of the problem with impotence is the pressure men put on themselves to perform. This exercise is designed to remove much of that pressure. Barring physical causes or medication, many times sexual arousal returns if you just relax and enjoy the process rather than try to force a response.

1. Create a safe time and place where you can talk over the experience of impotence. How do each of you feel about it? Don't be so careful or nice that you don't say all that you need to speak.

2. Have the male partner tell the other partner what internal thoughts and actions add to the feeling of pressure to perform.

3. Arrange at least three times in which you as a couple have a sexual experience in which erections do not play a part.

Help for Premature Ejaculation

GOALS OF THE EXERCISE

1. To facilitate couples working together to resolve premature ejaculation.
2. To help the male partner learn to delay ejaculation.

TYPES OF PROBLEMS THIS EXERCISE MAY BE MOST USEFUL FOR

- Communication
- Dependency
- Jealousy
- Loss of Love/Affection
- Sexual Dysfunction

SUGGESTIONS FOR PROCESSING THIS EXERCISE WITH THE COUPLE

1. What did you learn from this exercise?
2. Did the man have a stronger and longer lasting erection doing this exercise?
3. Which method worked best for you?

HELP FOR PREMATURE EJACULATION

The first thing to say about premature ejaculation is that many men ejaculate fairly quickly during intercourse. For some couples this becomes a problem and for others it never becomes an issue. Part of what makes it an issue for some couples is that the partner does not have a chance to have an orgasm through intercourse. This can be helped by ensuring that the partner is either sufficiently aroused to come quickly or has had an orgasm before intercourse through oral or manual stimulation. Here are two other experiments to try that may help.

1. The man must learn to attend to the sensations of an approaching orgasm and then slow down and stop moving before he gets to the point of no return. Many men feel they have to perform or keep moving to give their partners pleasure. Delaying ejaculation is a skill that can be learned. Work together to help your partner learn to slow down and enjoy the process. Make an agreement before you have intercourse that your partner will say when your partner must stop moving. Try this one time in the next week.

2. The man can masturbate to ejaculation an hour or so before intercourse. This often decreases the man's sensitivity or delays future ejaculations. Try this one time during the next week and find out whether it helps and is satisfying for both partners.

Initiation Week

GOAL OF THE EXERCISE

1. To change couples sexual initiation patterns.

TYPES OF PROBLEMS THIS EXERCISE MAY BE MOST USEFUL FOR

- Communication
- Jealousy
- Loss of Love/Affection
- Midlife Crisis
- Sexual Dysfunction

SUGGESTIONS FOR PROCESSING THIS EXERCISE WITH THE COUPLE

1. What did you learn from this exercise?
2. How did this challenge your ideas about yourself and your partner sexually?
3. Were you uncomfortable about initiating or having your partner initiate?

INITIATION WEEK

Most couples get in patterns and habits in which one partner initiates sex. How about trying something new?

1. The partner who usually doesn't initiate sex agrees to initiate one time in the next week, with the condition that it not be at bedtime.

2. After sex, spend at least 10 minutes discussing both or your experiences with this switch initiation of sex.

3. For the partner who initiated:

   • What was the most difficult thing about this for you?

   _____

   • How did you decide when to make your move?

   _____

   • What did you learn?

   _____

4. For the other:

   • Was this more like what you've been wanting?

   _____

   • What did you like about the way your partner initiated sex?

   _____

   • Were there any disadvantages to being in your position?

   _____

5. Would it help to do this exercise again?

Remember to bring completed work sheet to your next appointment.

Lightening Up about
Sexuality and Weight Gain

GOALS OF THE EXERCISE

1. To get the couples' focus off weight and onto sexual actions that they can change more easily.
2. To restore or enhance the couples' sexual life.

TYPES OF PROBLEMS THIS EXERCISE MAY BE MOST USEFUL FOR

- Communication
- Jealousy
- Loss of Love/Affection
- Midlife Crisis
- Sexual Dysfunction

SUGGESTIONS FOR PROCESSING THIS EXERCISE WITH THE COUPLE

1. Did you find that this exercise enhanced or restored any of your sexual life?
2. Did you find this exercise helpful in other ways?
3. How can you use this or similar ideas in the future or in other areas of your relationship?

LIGHTENING UP ABOUT SEXUALITY AND WEIGHT GAIN

> *When one partner tells the other that they are not sexually attracted to them because they have gained too much weight, there are ways of making some changes.*

Focusing on the weight issue is unproductive. Usually your partner is self-conscious or unhappy about his or her weight. Focusing on it only leads to more self-consciousness and unhappiness. Instead, focus on things that either one of you could do sexually. Doing some sexual or sensual things together often restores excitement to your sex life.

Tell your partner three things that you would like to do sexually with him or her that would be exciting. These can either be things you have done before or new things you would like to try. Remember that many parts of the body can be sensual and that the most important sex organ is between your ears. You can each list three or more things below:

_____

_____

_____

_____

_____

Discuss these things and find at least one of them that both of you are willing to try.

Make a commitment to trying this sexual experiment within the next week.

Remember to bring completed work sheet to your next appointment.

A Night to Remember

GOALS OF THE EXERCISE

1. To get the couples to reclaim the elements of their best remembered sexual experience.
2. To restore or enhance the couples' sexual life.

TYPES OF PROBLEMS THIS EXERCISE MAY BE MOST USEFUL FOR

- Communication
- Jealousy
- Loss of Love/Affection
- Midlife Crisis
- Sexual Dysfunction

SUGGESTIONS FOR PROCESSING THIS EXERCISE WITH THE COUPLE

1. Did you find that this exercise enhanced or restored any of your sexual life?
2. Did you find this exercise helpful in other ways?
3. How can you use this or similar ideas in the future or in other areas of your relationship?

A NIGHT TO REMEMBER

> *Many couples think wistfully about the good old days when their sex was passionate and plentiful. You may feel as if those days are gone forever or that you have to resort to more and more wild and radical activities to get as turned on as you used to. But it may be simpler than that.*

In this exercise, you are going to be the archeologists of your passion, uncovering previous experiences that you might dust off and reclaim for use in the present and the future.

Think of the best sexual experience you have had together as a couple

Each of you make your own list. List 3 things in each of these areas that helped make that sex good.

What you did:

1. _____

2. _____

3. _____

What your partner did:

1. _____

2. _____

3. _____

What environment were you in:

1. _____

2. _____

3. _____

What happened before, during, and after:

1. _____

2. _____

3. _____

Discuss these things and find at least one of them that both of you are willing to try.

Make a commitment to trying this sexual experiment within the next week.

Remember to bring completed work sheet to your next appointment.

Family, Stepfamily, and Parenting Problems

Wrestling with the Challenging Task of Parenting

GOALS OF THE EXERCISE

1. To normalize the experience of being overwhelmed by parenting at times.
2. To give the couple practice at taking breaks from parenting in a cooperative way.

TYPES OF PROBLEMS THIS EXERCISE MAY BE MOST USEFUL FOR

- Blended-Family Problems
- Communication
- Parenting Conflicts—Adolescents
- Parenting Conflicts—Children

SUGGESTIONS FOR PROCESSING THIS EXERCISE WITH THE COUPLE

1. What did you learn from this exercise?
2. What other ideas did you get about supporting each other as parents?
3. How did your children react?

WRESTLING WITH THE CHALLENGING TASK OF PARENTING

> *Everybody has their limits and kids sometimes can take you there and beyond. Before that happens, take a tip from the world of professional wrestling. Wait! Don't put a Full Nelson on them. Use the tag team approach and let your partner take over for a while.*

You may have seen tag-team wrestling. One member of the team is allowed in the ring at a time (at least, those are the rules). When that member gets into a tight spot, he or she is able to tag a team member outside the ring and that person takes over.

Discuss this concept with your partner and plan in advance how you will let your partner know you need to switch. You might want to discuss the advantages of waiting until the tag takes place before your partner enters the ring.

List five ways you will know it is time to get help.

_____

_____

_____

_____

_____

Track the times you make a switch.

Date: _____

What was happening: _____

How did you know it was time to switch?

_____

_____

_____

How did this make a difference?

_____

_____

_____

Date: _____

What was happening: _____

How did you know it was time to switch?

_____

_____

_____

How did this make a difference?

_____

_____

_____

Date: _____

What was happening: _____

How did you know it was time to switch?

_____

_____

_____

How did this make a difference?

_____

_____

_____

Remember to bring completed work sheet to your next appointment.

In-Law Problems

GOALS OF THE EXERCISE

1. To break unhelpful patterns of interactions between the couple and in-laws.
2. To give the couple or a partner a sense of empowerment in regard to the problem of intrusive in-laws.

TYPES OF PROBLEMS THIS EXERCISE MAY BE MOST USEFUL FOR

- Blended-Family Problems
- Communication

SUGGESTIONS FOR PROCESSING THIS EXERCISE WITH THE COUPLE

1. Did you notice any changes from your in-law(s) when you tried this approach?
2. Did you have fun with this exercise?
3. What have you learned from it?

IN-LAW PROBLEMS

> *Helpful family members who offer unwanted advice can put a major strain on a relationship. Changing the game can sometimes get them to back off.*

This exercise involves moving toward rather than running away from. Start tracking the unsolicited advice you get from your relative. At the same time, start calling at frequent intervals asking advice about increasingly mundane issues. Keep notes of all your contacts below:

Date: _____ Time: _____

Advice given:

_____

_____

_____

_____

Did you ask for it? _____

Who initiated the contact? _____

Date: _____ Time: _____

Advice given:

_____

_____

_____

_____

Did you ask for it? _____

Who initiated the contact? _____

Date: _____ Time: _____

Advice given:

_____

_____

_____

_____

Did you ask for it? _____

Who initiated the contact? _____

Date: _____ Time: _____

Advice given:

_____

_____

_____

_____

Did you ask for it? _____

Who initiated the contact? _____

Date: _____ Time: _____

Advice given:

_____

_____

_____

_____

Did you ask for it? _____

Who initiated the contact? _____

Remember to bring completed work sheet to your next appointment.

Get a Roommate

GOALS OF THE EXERCISE

1. To change unhelpful interactions between a stepparent and stepchildren.
2. To offer a helpful frame of reference for a stepparent in dealing more effectively with stepchildren.

TYPES OF PROBLEMS THIS EXERCISE MAY BE MOST USEFUL FOR

- Blended-Family Problems
- Communication
- Parenting Conflicts—Adolescents
- Parenting Conflicts—Children

SUGGESTIONS FOR PROCESSING THIS EXERCISE WITH THE COUPLE

1. Was this exercise helpful to you?
2. How did you change your approach with your stepchildren?
3. How did the stepchildren respond?
4. Did you (the other partner) notice any changes in your partner or your children from this exercise?

GET A ROOMMATE

> *Stepparents often have a difficult time defining their roles in dealing with the children of their new partner. This can be complicated further when the parent who doesn't live in the house is active in the upbringing of the children. This exercise suggests that you think of your role as "roommate." Even if you don't want to define your role this way, thinking in those terms may open some new ideas on your situation.*

Think of your stepchildren as your roommates.

What are five things you expect from a roommate?

_____

_____

_____

_____

_____

What do you do when a roommate doesn't fulfill his or her responsibilities?

_____

_____

_____

_____

_____

_____

_____

_____

_____

_____

List five responsibilities you have as a roommate.

_____

_____

_____

_____

_____

How do you and your roommates keep the health department from condemning your home?

_____

_____

_____

_____

_____

Remember to bring completed work sheet to your next appointment.

Circle the Wagons

GOALS OF THE EXERCISE

1. To strengthen the parental alliance.
2. To help the couple provide more consistent parenting.

TYPES OF PROBLEMS THIS EXERCISE MAY BE MOST USEFUL FOR

- Blended-Family Problems
- Communication
- Parenting Conflicts—Adolescents
- Parenting Conflicts—Children
- Physical Abuse
- Work/Home Role Strain

SUGGESTIONS FOR PROCESSING THIS EXERCISE WITH THE COUPLE

1. How was this different from your usual ways of handling parenting conflicts or disagreements?
2. Did the children notice the difference? Did they respond any differently?
3. Were there any glitches or problems that you need to smooth out?

CIRCLE THE WAGONS

At times, being parents can put stress on any relationship and some children seem to have a knack for homing in on the issues where parents disagree. Disagreements about consequences or rules sometimes lead to the child getting his or her own way and subverting the parental authority in a way that leaves both parents dissatisfied. Here are some ideas for handling this kind of situation.

What are five rules or consequences that you frequently disagree about?

_____

_____

_____

_____

_____

List five early signs that would let you know that a disagreement is brewing.

_____

_____

_____

_____

_____

When you notice a disagreement starting, inform the child that you are having a summit conference and retreat to a place where you can discuss the matter privately. If that is impossible at the moment, inform the child that the two of you will need to discuss the matter and you will get back to him or her.

Use the rest of the page to make notes of any conferences that you have held so you can discuss you experiences with your therapist.

Remember to bring completed work sheet to your next appointment.

Section IV

Reproducible Forms and Brochures

Guidelines for Couples' Communication

GET SPECIFIC

Use videotalk. Describe what you are talking about so clearly that your partner could imagine seeing or hearing it on a videotape. If the person can't picture what you are saying or imagine hearing it, you aren't being specific enough to ensure your message will be heard. There is too much room for misinterpretation when you use vague words. Avoid giving your opinions, interpretations, or generalizations when you are having communication problems. They are invitations to misunderstandings and conflicts.

AVOID THE BLAME GAME OR DECIDING WHO IS REALLY RIGHT

Relationships are either win/win or lose/lose. If either of you loses, you both lose, because the relationship suffers. While it is tempting to get righteous or prove your partner wrong, it sets up a barrier to understanding and listening. Instead, imagine for a moment that there is another way of seeing the situation that might be different.

BE ACCOUNTABLE FOR WHAT YOU SAY OR DO

Each of us has a choice about what we say and do, no matter how we feel. Don't excuse your behavior or blame it on others or your childhood.

STICK WITH THE RECENT PAST WHEN YOU TALK ABOUT PROBLEMS

It is harder to change the past than the present and the future. People forget and disagree about what happened in the distant past.

ACKNOWLEDGE YOUR PARTNER'S FEELINGS AND POINTS OF VIEW

Listening to and acknowledging the other person's feelings and points of view can bypass many arguments and misunderstandings. Don't try to correct them or rebut their points of view or feelings. Just listen. See if you can understand what the other person is trying to communicate. You don't have to agree with what they are saying, but don't dismiss or minimize their feelings or tell them what is wrong with them for feeling that way.

NOTICE AND GIVE YOUR PARTNER AND YOUR RELATIONSHIP CREDIT FOR THE GOOD STUFF

It's all too easy to focus on the problems in relationships. Did your partner talk to you about something he or she would usually have avoided? Give them credit for that, even if you are upset about what they said. Did you two talk out something that you usually would have gotten stuck on? Mention it and acknowledge it to each other.

BREAK YOUR PATTERNS

It takes two to tango, so start doing the fox trot and find out what happens. Change your part of any pattern that isn't working. Do anything that is not cruel, unethical, or distasteful to your partner that would be different from what you usually do in the situation. Remember: Insanity is doing the same thing over and over again and expecting different results. You can change your part of the pattern and invite your partner to change.

How to Solve
Relationship Problems

If It Ain't Broke . . .

If things are going well in some area, you don't have to change that area or doubt yourself or the relationship. Determine what is working and do more of that.

Stop Listening to Experts

These days, you can find yourself doing something kind or compassionate for your partner and wonder if you are really being "co-dependent." Or reading a magazine article and suddenly deciding that your relationship doesn't really make it according to the guidelines you are reading. You are your own relationship expert. Trust your intuition and your common sense. Don't let outside experts (not just the ones in magazines or on television talk shows, also your well-intentioned friends, coworkers, or relatives) talk you out of something you like or into something that you know isn't right for you.

Do Something Different

They say that the only difference between a rut and a grave is the dimensions, and some couples have gotten into pretty deep ruts. Try changing anything you do in the relationship when you have problems (keep it ethical and safe, of course). If you usually argue in the bedroom, go into the kitchen and have the same discussion by writing it out on paper to one another and passing notes. If you usually fall asleep to the evening news, go bowling one night. Break out of your usual ruts by doing something completely out of character for you. If you continue to do what you usually do, you'll probably continue to get the usual responses and results.

FIND A DIFFERENT WAY TO LOOK AT THINGS

There's an old saying: Nothing is as dangerous as an idea when it is the only one you have. We are all prisoners of our limited points of view and we have a tendency to think our point of view is the only correct way of seeing things, especially when we are upset. So, when you are stuck or unhappy, find another way of looking at it. Think of the situation from another angle. For example, how would you be thinking of this situation if it was your child or your best friend instead of your spouse or partner?

Creating or Renewing Intimacy

Intimacy is personal for every relationship. Find out what helps each of you feel or sustain closeness and affection in your relationship. Here are some hints about some areas to examine and things to try to create, enhance, or sustain intimacy.

SPENDING TIME TOGETHER

Most people who feel close to one another spend a certain amount of time alone with one another. In busy times, with the demands of children and work, some couples find that they leave their time together as the last thing on their agenda. It might be important to put some special effort into scheduling or carving out some time regularly to spend with one another without distractions.

GET PHYSICAL

Most couples who report intimacy find that they touch each other in little ways when they are together: holding hands, sitting close, giving hugs when greeting or parting, touching the other person's elbow or shoulder when talking, and so on. In more private settings, there is more sexual touching. Has the touch or physical contact gone out of your relationship? Can you begin to reinstate it with simple gestures, like giving each other backrubs or holding hands while watching television? That might go a long way toward restoring or sustaining feelings of closeness.

BE VULNERABLE

Telling each other things that are risky to say, because you might be hurt or criticized by the other person, is a way to create or restore intimacy. Couples often share their hopes, dreams, and vulnerable feelings early on during courtship, but less so as time goes on. Many a

180

midlife crisis was brought on by one partner feeling that he or she could no longer share deep, vulnerable feelings with their partner. Take a chance with your partner by sharing something a bit risky. It could open the door to intimacy.

DROP JUDGMENTS AND COMMUNICATE COMPASSION AND ADMIRATION

One of the barriers to intimacy is feeling that one's partner doesn't like or respect you or that you are being judged. Try dropping your critical feelings about your partner and developing some compassion or understanding, or acceptance of quirks or nondestructive habits. Does he love baseball? Instead of belittling his passion, try supporting him in his interest. Does she cry at movies? Don't scoff and tell her she is being too sentimental, but give her the message that she is okay and you admire her for crying when she sees sad things.

Pocket Emergency Guidelines

Do Something Different

Don't keep doing the same thing. Change any pattern that is under your influence. Don't do anything dangerous or unethical, but get creative. Blow your partner's stereotype of you. Think about what you would normally do next and do something different.

Get Specific (Use Action Talk Rather Than Blaming or Vague Words)

Don't give theories or use general words. Describe the situation in a more objective way, stating what you can see or hear.

Practice Compassionate Listening

Even if you feel attacked or don't understand your partner's actions or words, imagine that they are feelings scared or hurt at the moment when there are problems. Try getting into their shoes or skin and imagining or trying to understand how they are seeing or feeling in this situation. Be sure that you understand and that your partner feels understood before you respond.

Don't Do Anything Drastic or Make Hasty Decisions

In the heat of the moment, we might make decisions or take action out of the anger, hurt, fear, or frustration. Take a few deep breaths and wait to calm down and get some distance before you make any hasty decisions or take impulsive actions. If necessary, take a "time out" well before you say or do something you will later regret.

THINK!

While emotions provide important information when you are making decisions, doing what feels right at the moment will often cause problems.

USE THE PAST

Think about what has worked in similar situations in the past and consider how you can use that to help you this time.

PLAN AHEAD

Write down any notes that you think might help. You may want to include such things as phone numbers you can call or words you want to use in a tough situation.

Getting Over an Affair

People and relationships can and do heal from affairs. While each situation is unique, there are some general principles you may find helpful in moving on from such a painful and conflict-filled situation.

For the person who has had the affair:

Be accountable. Don't give excuses that claim you had no choice in the matter (like "She came on to me," "You were unfaithful years ago, so I was justified," or "We weren't having enough sex.").

Acknowledge what you did. You lied and your credibility is in doubt to your partner. Now is the time to step up and tell the truth. That doesn't mean to go into all the details, but to own up to your betrayal.

Take reasonable measures to rebuild trust (e.g., be where you say you're going to be and be there when you say you will). Be extra careful not to hide anything about what you are doing, however trivial it may seem to you or however much you are afraid it might hurt your partner. You don't have to share every passing feeling, but don't lie about your activities.

Apologize and offer to make amends, if possible. Acknowledge that what you did hurt your partner and offer your apologies. Ask your partner what you could do to make amends, if anything.

For the person who has been betrayed:

Don't badmouth your partner to your family or friends. They will, of course, side with you. It will come back to haunt you if you stay together, because your friends and family will be alienated from your partner or critical of you for getting back together with him or her. That doesn't mean you shouldn't seek support from your friends or family. Just be careful about how you talk about it.

Don't stalk or check up on your partner constantly. Either the person is going to be trustworthy or not. You'll eventually find out if you are being betrayed again. You can take reasonable precautions and do random checks to reassure yourself, but don't make it your waking preoccupation.

Don't ask detailed questions. Often you'll hear things that will haunt you for years, images that you will find hard to forget or get over. Once you know the broad outlines of what happened, let it rest for awhile. If you find you are still haunted by those questions, try doing a ritual (see below) to help let it go. Or have your partner write out or record all the details and put the record of the affair in a safety deposit box and give the key to a friend with instructions not to let you have the key for a year. If you still feel the need to know, go and look at the material after a year. Most people don't want to see it by then, as they have some distance and don't want to open the whole painful mess again.

Do a ritual of letting go or moving on. This involves symbolically letting some emotion or situation go by physically getting rid of something that represents or symbolizes the unfinished business. For example, you might write a letter about everything you feel or want to say about the affair and then burn the pages you have written. Or you might get a picture of the person your partner had the affair with, tear it up and throw it in the ocean. One person got a keychain with the name of the person her husband had an affair with on it and drove back and forth over the keychain with her car to let go of many of her angry feelings toward that woman. Find something physical that represents the unfinished feelings or situation and do something symbolic of releasing it.

Dealing with a Partner or Spouse with a Chemical Abuse Problem

Don't Argue Diagnoses

One of the major hassles that couples get in regarding drug and alcohol problems is that one person tries to convince the other that he or she is really drug addicted or alcoholic. That is fine if your partner is open to accepting this label, but much of the time he or she isn't convinced the problem is that serious or merits that diagnosis. Contrary to what you may have read or heard, many people deal successfully with substance abuse problems without ever accepting the label of addiction or alcoholism. The more important issue is to deal with the drinking or drug-taking behavior and its consequences. You can spend crucial time and energy on this more peripheral issue and alienate your partner in the process. Stick to what is important. Choose your battles wisely.

Talk It Over

Often the first step is to have a heart-to-heart talk with your partner about substance abuse and how you see it affecting your relationship and your family. State in no uncertain terms what you are asking your partner to do. Ask if there is anything you can do to help. After you have done this and have met any reasonable requests for assistance, accept that you have gone as far as you can to directly change your partner's abuse. If he or she doesn't make changes, you need to take steps designed more to take care of yourself than to change the behavior. Some people respond to consequences presented by the partner, but if you are providing consequences, don't do it with the intention of getting the user to change. It will usually be seen as manipulation.

SET CLEAR BOUNDARIES AND MAKE SPECIFIC AGREEMENTS REGARDING THE PROBLEMS RELATED TO THE SUBSTANCE USE

A better approach than arguing about labels is to set clear boundaries for what is acceptable and unacceptable or dangerous behavior and stick to those boundaries. Clear means setting the boundaries in a specific way so that you and your partner both know when those boundaries are honored and when they are violated. For example, if your partner routinely tells you that he or she will be home at a certain time and shows up late, make sure that the boundary is clear. "If you are going to be any more than 15 minutes later than you said you'd be, please call telling me what time you expect to be home." Or, if your partner has been missing work due to drinking, focus the boundary setting on getting to work consistently and make the limits clear and unmistakable. "If you miss any more days of work, I think you are putting your job at risk and hurting our family finances. I would like you to do what you need to do to get to work every day for the next month." In many cases, if you focus on the drinking itself, you are likely to get into an unproductive argument. But in some situations, you might be able to make a clear agreement about the amount or frequency of drinking.

DON'T MAKE EXCUSES FOR YOUR PARTNER'S SUBSTANCE USE

From decades of experience with drug and alcohol problems, we have learned that one of the things that can inadvertently keep these problems going much longer than they otherwise would have lasted is if one partner develops a habit of making excuses for their partner's drug or alcohol use or buffering that person from the consequences of their behavior. If they are hung over, don't call in to work for them saying that they are sick if you can't wake them up. Don't let them off the hook for inappropriate behavior just because they have been using drugs or alcohol. For example, if the person gets violent when drunk, don't explain the violence away as a result of the alcohol. Hold the person accountable for the violence (and the alcohol use).

TAKE CARE OF YOURSELF

When you travel on an airplane, they make an announcement during the initial safety orientation. "If there is an emergency, oxygen masks will drop from the overhead compartment. If you are traveling with small children, put your oxygen mask on first, then assist your child with putting his or hers on." Why is this? Because if you pass out, your child will be very unlikely to help you, but you could help him or her if they passed out first. In a similar way, it may be important for you to take care of yourself first in situations in which drugs and alcohol have come to affect you and your family. What is the oxygen mask for you? Do you need to have a separate checking or savings account in order to take care of yourself and your children? Do you need to go to an Al-Anon meeting while you are dealing with your partner's problem? Do you need to make sure you exercise or take vitamins regularly? Don't get so focused on your partner's problem that you neglect to care for yourself.

TALK WITH THE KIDS

Kids usually know exactly what is going on with their parents. There is a well-known phrase referring to the presence of alcohol problems in a family which aren't acknowledged or talked about: There's an elephant in the living room that nobody talks about. If the problem becomes serious enough, it may be time to talk with the children and explain the situation. Beware of labels and psychological theories. Just straightforwardly explain the problem that you or your partner is having with substance abuse and the plan you have to tackle it. Answer any of the children's questions as honestly as possible (without revealing anything inappropriate for children to know or blaming anyone).

Preventing or Dealing with Violence in a Relationship

BREAKING THE SECRECY, SILENCE, AND SHAME

One of the things that supports violence in a relationship is keeping it secret. Some people who are battered or hit think that somehow there is something about them that brings on the violence or that it says something shameful about them. We are finding out that many more people, men and women, are subjected to violence in the home than we ever imagined. If you can, let someone know. This is not only for the person being hurt, but for the person who is doing the hurting. Violence can often be handled more effectively when you admit that it is happening and get help and support from others to change it.

MINIMIZING VIOLENCE

Another thing that can keep violence going is for either partner or both of you to dismiss it as trivial or to minimize it. It is a natural human tendency to play down the difficult or embarrassing things that happen. One way to counteract this tendency is to record the incident of violence on tape or through writing just after it occurs. It is still fresh in your mind and harder to play down. Later, when you have dismissed it or remembered that it wasn't so bad, you can check your sense of it with the record you have made.

BEING ACCOUNTABLE

We all have choices about our behavior, no matter what the circumstances. Often in situations of violence, the person who strikes out denies this responsibility by blaming the violence on the other person or on things beyond their control ("She kept at me, so I hit her," or

"I have a temper, just like my mother. I can't help hitting when I get angry."). An important step in stopping violence is for each partner to take responsibility for his or her behavior and not to offer excuses that claim they have no choice about what they do.

LOOK TO THE TIMES WHEN VIOLENCE WAS LIKELY BUT YOU AVOIDED IT AS A MODEL

Most couples with a history of violence also have a history of preventing violence. Examine times when one or both of you felt there was a likelihood of violence, but something one or both of you did prevented it. Did you walk away for a time? Did you stop talking and just sit in silence for a time? Did you calm yourself down in some way? was someone else in the house or nearby? Find the elements that helped prevent the eruption of violence and use those as a model for how to prevent or avoid it in the future.

DEVELOP A PREVENTION PLAN

Even if you can't identify previous solutions, can you sit down together and plan for how to prevent violence in the future? Experiment with things that you think would be helpful. Talk over the potential pitfalls or failures of such a plan so that it is as realistic as possible. Write it down so you can consult it when it is needed. Make an agreement that you'll both stick to the plan when the time comes.

MAKE A LIST OF WARNING SIGNS

Most couples can give a list of signs that violence is coming. Is it when one person's voice volume gets loud? Is it when you get into an argument late at night? Is it when one person starts to call the other names? Is it right after taking a drink and then starting a discussion? Identify warning signs of violence and then put the prevention plan or things that worked previously to avoid violence into practice.

MAKE AN ESCAPE PLAN

Even the best of plans can go amiss. We know from research that many people stay in relationships in which there is ongoing violence. So, it's best to prepare an escape plan for the times when violence erupts. Prepare a list of options for escape. Hide an extra set of car and house keys someplace where you can get to them if you have to run out of the house (under the back step or at a neighbors). Stash some money or a credit card. Pack a bag for you or you and the kids. Have the number of the battered women's shelter or a hotel handy. Post a list of emergency numbers for the police, the shelter, the ambulance, your counselor, the AA sponsor, and so on.

DON'T TRY TO SOLVE PROBLEMS WHEN UNDER THE INFLUENCE

Drugs and alcohol are often a component of violence in relationships. Even if some issue is pressing, put off discussion of it until both of you are sober. If there is never such a time, it is a sign that you need help.

Solving Sexual Problems

WHEN YOU'RE HOT, YOU'RE HOT AND WHEN YOU'RE NOT, YOU'RE NOT

Don't try to force yourself to feel sexual excitement when you are not feeling it. Sometimes when men lose their erections, they become self-conscious and try to force what had been a natural process of sexual excitement. This usually has the exact opposite effect. The same goes for women, lubrication, and sexual excitement. Sometimes the lack of sexual excitement may be just temporary or due to the situation. In that case, just accepting this lack of excitement can help you get through this time. The next time, things will probably work just fine. Or the lack of sexual excitement may be due to more long-term factors, such as a medical condition or medications that interfere with arousal or response. Or it may be an indication of boredom or problems in your sexual relationship or your relationship in general. Regardless of the reason for the lack of arousal, the suggestion remains the same. Don't try to force yourself to become aroused.

LET YOUR PARTNER KNOW WHAT FEELS GOOD (AND WHAT DOESN'T)

Think of sex as a bit like backscratching. Your partner could have no way of knowing what feels good to you at the moment unless you let him or her know. This is sometimes hard for people in the realm of sex because they are not use to speaking openly about sexual matters, but it is crucial to break that silence and speak up if you want to enhance your sexual relationship.

GET CREATIVE

Get out of ruts. Try new positions, new locations, talk, clothes, toys, and so on. Read each other fantasies you have found in books or magazines or written out of your imagination.

ASK FOR WHAT YOU WANT, BUT DON'T DEMAND IT

People don't usually respond well in sexual situations when they are feeling uncomfortable or forced to participate in something they don't like. So, make sure you are not coercing or forcing your partner to do things they don't want to do. At the same time, sometimes people don't speak up about what they desire or would like to try because they are afraid their partner wouldn't like it or would disapprove. You can at least bring the subject up to your partner and let them know there is no demand, but an interest in trying some sexual behavior.

SCHEDULE TIME

Don't always leave it until late at night or assume it will happen spontaneously. You may have to schedule time out of your busy work, social or family life for sexual encounters. Again, the key here is to take the pressure off. You are scheduling time to allow sexual interactions, but if the timing or the situation isn't right, just use that time to reconnect in any way you can. You might just give each other backrubs, or talk, or snuggle. If sex happens, great! If not, relax and enjoy this special time together.

FANTASIES AND DESIRES DON'T NECESSARILY EQUAL IDENTITY OR LEAD TO BEHAVIOR

Just because you fantasize about things, it doesn't necessarily indicate that you want to act those things out or have them happen in the real world. You may fantasize about being raped or having sex with someone of the same sex, but you may never want to experience that in reality.

This can also hold true for your sexual identity. Many people have attractions to people of the same sex, but don't define themselves as homosexual. Likewise, sometimes people who are homosexual have attractions to people of the opposite sex, but still think of themselves as gay or lesbian. Your sexual identity is partly a matter of where you feel comfortable and what your attractions are, but it is mainly a function of how you choose to define yourself. You may not have much choice about what or who turns you on, but your identity is much more a matter of choice and preference. Some people live their whole lives being primarily attracted to one sex, yet define themselves in a very different way. Call it denial or whatever you will, sexual identity is a political act and each person must sort out their own politics.

You *can* let yourself feel, fantasize, or think anything you experience sexually. Your experience does not have to determine your choices in life or define you.

193

MEDICATIONS, ALCOHOL/DRUGS AND MEDICAL CONDITIONS CAN AFFECT SEXUAL DESIRE AND RESPONSES

In small amounts, drugs or alcohol may help you relax inhibitions, but in larger amounts they can interfere with sexual functioning. Medications can also interfere with sexual desire or functioning. If you are using medications and experiencing problems of desire or functioning, check with a physician or pharmacist who is knowledgeable in such matters and make adjustments in your prescription if necessary. If you are regularly using significant amounts of drugs or alcohol, try decreasing and then stopping your substance use and find out if your desire or response returns. If it doesn't, there may be a medical condition that is affecting your desire. Again, check with a physician about these matters.

IN SEARCH OF THE BIG O

Don't get so hung up on the goal that you ignore or rush the process. Trying too hard to have an orgasm can prevent you from having one or enjoying it when it arrives. On the other hand, if you never or rarely have orgasms, you can make adjustments so that this becomes a more regular part of your sexual experience. Use the other suggestions here to enhance the likelihood of experiencing orgasms.

What about premature ejaculation? Slow down, stop moving, pay attention to when his orgasm is approaching. Many men feel they have to perform or keep moving to give their partners pleasure. Delaying ejaculation is a skill that can be learned. Work together to help him learn to slow down and enjoy the process.

What about having simultaneous orgasms? It is possible, again with good communication and with taking the pressure off. Some couples have this experience quite regularly and others have such different timing that it is unlikely they will coordinate orgasms.

Train Your Therapist

TELL YOUR THERAPIST WHAT WORKS AND HAS WORKED FOR YOU

Each person and couple is unique. You can help your therapist by teaching him the style and questions he or she uses that work best for you as an individual and as a couple. That does not mean that you run the therapy. The therapist does have some expertise and good reasons for doing what he or she is doing, but a good therapist also has some room for flexibility. If you have been in counseling before and found some aspect or method particularly helpful, let your therapist know about that.

LET YOUR THERAPIST KNOW WHEN HE OR SHE DOES SOMETHING RIGHT

Therapy can be a difficult and challenging field of work. Your therapist sees people when they are at their most stressed, and sometimes most impatient. Sometimes the therapist doesn't know whether he or she has been helpful, because people don't return or change takes some time. So, most therapists appreciate hearing that they have done something that worked or was helpful. This can also make your therapy experience more productive, since your therapist will have your feedback to guide him or her in future attempts to help you.

TELL YOUR THERAPIST YOUR EXPECTATIONS

If you attend therapy expecting to go back to your childhood to find the roots of the problem and your therapist focuses on the present, someone is bound to be frustrated if that expectation isn't brought up and discussed before you proceed. Also, you might indicate how long you had anticipated you would attend therapy, and how often, to make sure you and the therapist are on the same track.

TELL YOUR THERAPIST WHAT DOESN'T WORK

Like telling your therapist your expectations and letting them know what has worked or is helping, letting him or her know when something isn't helping is important. This includes what is happening at home as well as during your therapy sessions. This gives the opportunity for mid-course corrections in the therapy process.

TELL YOUR THERAPIST YOUR OBJECTIONS

Some people think that they shouldn't speak up about their worries or objections to their therapist's suggestions, but a free and frank discussion about any misgiving helps your therapist deal with your concerns and make any adjustments to ensure a higher likelihood of success.

ASK QUESTIONS

About the therapy process, fees, any suggestions or methods, the therapist's training and qualifications, etc. Anything you are curious about. If it gets too personal or the therapist considers the questions intrusive or inappropriate, he or she will let you know.

DEMAND THAT YOUR THERAPIST SPEAK EVERYDAY ENGLISH (OR SPANISH OR WHATEVER LANGUAGE YOU SPEAK)

All professions have jargon and buzzwords. If your therapist suggests an MMPI to check out whether you have MPD or ADHD, you have a perfect right to have a translation into language you understand.

Relationship Rescue: Ten Methods for Resolving Relationship Crises

This material is designed to help you quickly break through relationship impasses and resolve crises. Use any of these methods that make sense to you and that work.

CHANGE YOUR USUAL CONFLICT PATTERNS OR STYLE

If you usually get loud, soften your voice volume. If you usually run away or withdraw during an argument, stay put. If you usually try to argue your point of view with a lawyer's precision and aggressiveness, just state your feelings in the matter and let it rest. If you usually interrupt your partner's talking to rebut or refute what they are saying, just listen until they are done talking, then repeat what they have said back to them and ask whether you have understood what their point is or feelings are. If you usually point your finger during an argument, sit on your hands while you are having the argument.

Or you might try changing the mode of expression you usually use to communicate. If you are talking, switch to a piece of paper and write out what you have to say. Or record it into a tape recorder and ask your partner to listen to it in another room.

Another way to change your usual conflict patterns or style is to change the location or the timing. Instead of arguing in the living room, go to the front seat of the car or a restaurant to argue. If you usually argue late at night, make an appointment for the next afternoon and have the argument then. Or limit the argument to 10 minutes using the kitchen timer and then take a break for 10 minutes, getting some physical distance from one another and remaining silent. Then argue another 10 minutes, followed by another 10 minutes of silence. Continue this pattern until the issue is resolved or you both agree to stop.

DO A 180: CHANGE YOUR USUAL PURSUER-DISTANCER PATTERN

This is a variation on the last method, but it is more specific. Most couples fall into a typical pattern of who pursues and who withdraws, both in the relationship and during conflicts. Figure out which part of the pattern you usually play out and change your style (from the person who withdraws to the person who stays or pursues or vice versa). Both of you can make these changes or either one of you.

CATCH YOUR PARTNER DOING SOMETHING RIGHT

Make note of and speak to your partner about everything that you can think of to give them credit for in the recent past. Tell them about times when you felt cared about, helped or understood by them and the specific things that they did that led you to feel that way. Mention things that they did that you admired or were pleasantly surprised about. Catch them doing or almost doing something you want them to do differently and praise them for it. Notice when they do something during an argument that seems more fair, more compassionate or friendly or that helps you to resolve things. (Hint: You can also catch yourself doing something right and silently give yourself credit. Note that righteousness is not encouraged. Rather, notice when you are being flexible, compassionate and understanding.)

UNPACK VAGUE, BLAMING, AND LOADED WORDS INTO VIDEOTALK (ACTION DESCRIPTIONS)

Notice what words you are using that get a rise out of your partner and find a way to use less loaded or provocative words or phrases. For example, you might find that when you say things like, "You're being selfish," or "You're just like your father," your partner reacts badly. The simplest way to defuse such phrases and words is to translate them into action descriptions or what could be called "videotalk." Videotalk means to use words that describe what you could see and hear on a videotape, rather than using more vague or judgmental words. So, instead of saying, "Well, when you were judging me, I got defensive." You could try saying, "When you pointed your finger at me and said I was immature, I got defensive."

CHANGE YOUR COMPLAINTS INTO "ACTION REQUESTS"

Probably the most crucial area to use videotalk is in telling your partner what is bothering you about the relationship or what they are doing with or around you. Instead of indicting the person for personality flaws or having the wrong feelings, describing their behavior in videotalk usually seems less blaming and is more likely to give them a hint about what they might change to make things better.

MAKE A SPECIFIC CHANGE PLAN

Often we do better in making changes if we sit and plan a strategy of action, write it down and check back on what we have written down on a regular basis. This can be done with or without your partner. In making such a plan, it is important to include specific actions that you or your partner or both of you are going to take, a timeline for taking such actions or a commitment to how frequently you will take such actions and a plan for how and when to check back on the plan to see if it's working or to make adjustments.

FOCUS ON HOW YOU (NOT YOUR PARTNER) CAN CHANGE AND TAKE RESPONSIBILITY FOR MAKING THAT CHANGE

Even if your partner is the source of the problem, this method involves you assuming responsibility for making changes. This is based on the idea that people are responsive to changes around them. If you stop doing the tango and start doing the fox trot, your partner will have a harder time doing the old tango steps. So, figure out places in the usual course of things that go wrong in which you have a moment of choice to do something different and new that isn't harmful or destructive.

BLOW YOUR PARTNER'S STEREOTYPE OF YOU

Sometimes the people we live with get a stereotyped impression of who we are. And we confirm that by always playing our typical roles. Figure out what your partner's stereotype of you is (you never do any work around the house, or you are always critical when they want to watch football) and make a determined effort to shatter their expectations. Surprise yourself and them by doing something that would be entirely out of character for you (but again, make sure it is not destructive or mean spirited).

COMPASSIONATE LISTENING

Sometimes the simplest solution is to just stop and listen to what your partner is saying and imagine how he or she could be feeling that way or seeing things in that light. Don't try to defend yourself, correct their perceptions or talk them out of their feelings. Just put yourself in their position and try to hear how they understand, interpret and feel about the situation and imagine how you would feel or act if your were seeing things that way. Express that understanding to them and let them know how difficult it must be for them, given how they are feeling about the situation.

When you are stuck in a relationship problem, things can seem hopeless. This handout has some ideas and methods you can use to get yourself unstuck. If problems persist or you find yourself too discouraged to even consider these methods, it is wise to seek the help of a marriage or relationship counselor.

Dealing with the Death of a Child

It is said that the worst thing that can befall a parent is the death of their child. It certainly seems to be reflected in the alarmingly high divorce rate among parents who have lost a child. Divorce is not inevitable and many marriages do make it through this terrible and challenging experience. One of the major challenges seems to be coming to terms with differences in grieving styles. One partner may wish to stop talking about the child's death and the other may want to talk a great deal about it to process the grief, thus creating further stress at an already stressful time.

Acknowledge that each person has his or her style and timing. Some people like to hold on to the child and some prefer to let go. Some prefer to speak about their grief or cry about it and others feel numb or want to process it in silence. There is no right way or wrong way to deal with death.

Likewise with books and pamphlets about the grieving process. Nobody can tell anyone else the right way to, the right timing for or the proper stages for grief. Even if you don't think you are doing it correctly, are numb, are "overly" upset, feel relief or feel guilty, these can all be part of a "normal" grief process. Don't let anyone tell you what is right for you if it doesn't fit for you.

Some people find that making a donation, doing public speaking, or working to raise public awareness or make some changes in the world can be ways to give the child's death some meaning and find some higher purpose to cope with the loss. What would give your child's death some meaning? What contribution could his or her death, as terrible as it is, make to others?

Some find that instead of letting the child go, they can imagine that the child is there to give them advice and consolation at this time of grief (and perhaps for years into the future). Friends and family, even professionals, will often urge you to say good-bye. Perhaps it would be best for you to say hello again. What would your child say to you now to help you cope with the situation?

Generic Assignment Form

ACTION PLANS/IDEAS TO CONSIDER

Your Name: _____ Your Address: _____

Phone Number: _____ City, State, Zip: _____

Next Appointment Time/Date: _____ Today's Date: _____

References

Hudson, P., & O'Hanlon, W. (1991). *Rewriting love stories: Brief marital therapy.* New York: Norton.

O'Hanlon, B., & Hudson, P. (1995). *Love is a verb: How to stop analyzing your relationship and start making it great!* New York: Norton.

O'Hanlon, S., & O'Hanlon, B. (1998) Love is a noun (Except when it's a verb): A solution-oriented approach to intimacy. In L. Sperry & J. Carlson (Eds.), *The intimate couple.* Washington, DC: Brunner/Mazel.

Schultheis, G. (1998). *Brief therapy homework planner.* New York: Wiley.

Practice *Planners* ™

Practice Planners™ offer mental health professionals a full array of practice management tools. These easy-to-use resources include *Treatment Planners*, which cover all the necessary elements for developing formal treatment plans, including detailed problem definitions, long-term goals, short-term objectives, therapeutic interventions, and DSM-IV diagnoses; *Homework Planners* featuring behaviorally-based, ready-to-use assignments which are designed for use between sessions; and *Documentation Sourcebooks* that provide all the forms and records that therapists need to run their practice.

For more information on the titles listed below, fill out and return this form to: John Wiley & Sons, Attn: M.Fellin, 605 Third Avenue, New York, NY 10158.

Name _____

Address _____

Address _____

City/State/Zip _____

Telephone _____ Email _____

Please send me more information on:

❑ The Complete Psychotherapy Treatment Planner / 176pp / 0-471-11738-2 / $39.95
❑ The Child and Adolescent Psychotherapy Treatment Planner / 240pp / 0-471-15647-7 / $39.95
❑ The Chemical Dependence Treatment Planner / 208pp / 0-471-23795-7 / $39.95
❑ The Continuum of Care Treatment Planner / 208pp / 0-471-19568-5 / $39.95
❑ The Couples Therapy Treatment Planner / 208pp / 0-471-24711-1 / $39.95
❑ The Employee Assistance (EAP) Treatment Planner / 176pp / 0-471-24709-X / $39.95
❑ The Pastoral Counseling Treatment Planner / 208pp / 0-471-25416-9 / $39.95
❑ The Older Adult Psychotherapy Treatment Planner / 176pp / 0-471-29574-4 / $39.95
❑ The Behavioral Medicine Treatment Planner / 176pp / 0-471-31923-6 / $39.95
❑ The Complete Adult Psychotherapy Treatment Planner, Second Edition / 224pp / 0-471-31922-4 / $39.95
❑ TheraScribe® 3.0 for Windows®: The Computerized Assistant to Psychotherapy Treatment Planning Software / 0-471-18415-2 / $450.00 (For network pricing, call 1-800-0655x4708)
❑ TheraBiller™ w/TheraScheduler: The Computerized Mental Health Office Manager Software / 0-471-17102-2 / $599.00 (For network pricing, call 1-800-0655x4708)
❑ Brief Therapy Homework Planner / 256pp / 0-471-24611-5 / $49.95
❑ The Couples & Family Clinical Documentation Sourcebook / 208pp / 0-471-25234-4 / $49.95
❑ The Child & Adolescent Homework Planner / 256pp / 0-471-32366-7 / $49.95
❑ The Psychotherapy Documentation Primer / 224pp / 0-471-28990-6 / $39.95
❑ The Clinical Documentation Sourcebook / 256pp / 0-471-17934-5 / $49.95
❑ The The Forensic Documentation Sourcebook / 224pp / 0-471-25459-2 / $75.00
❑ The Chemical Dependence Treatment Documentation Sourcebook / 304pp / 0-471-31285-1 / $49.95
❑ The Child Clinical Documentation Sourcebook / 256pp / 0-471-29111-0 / $49.95

Order the above products through your local bookseller, or by calling 1-800-225-5945, from 8:30 a.m. to 5:30 p.m., est. You can also order via our web site: www.wiley.com/practiceplanners

WILEY
Publishers Since 1807

About the Disk

INTRODUCTION

The forms on the enclosed disk are saved in Microsoft Word for Windows version 7.0. In order to use the forms, you will need to have word processing software capable of reading Microsoft Word for Windows version 7.0 files.

SYSTEM REQUIREMENTS

- IBM PC or compatible computer
- 3.5" floppy disk drive
- Windows 95 or later
- Microsoft Word for Windows version 7.0 or later or other word processing software capable of reading Microsoft Word for Windows 7.0 files.

NOTE: Many popular word processing programs are capable of reading Microsoft Word for Windows 7.0 files. However, users should be aware that a slight amount of formatting might be lost when using a program other than Microsoft Word. If your word processor cannot read Microsoft Word for Windows 7.0 files, unformatted text files have been provided in the TXT directory on the floppy disk.

HOW TO INSTALL THE FILES ONTO YOUR COMPUTER

To install the files, follow the instructions below.

1. Insert the enclosed disk into the floppy disk drive of your computer.
2. From the Start Menu, choose **Run.**
3. Type **A:\SETUP** and press **OK.**
4. The opening screen of the installation program will appear. Press **OK** to continue.

5. The default destination directory is C:\COUPLES. If you wish to change the default destination, you may do so now.
6. Press **OK** to continue. The installation program will copy all files to your hard drive in the C:\COUPLES or user-designated directory.

USING THE FILES

Loading Files

To use the word processing files, launch your word processing program. Select **File, Open** from the pull-down menu. Select the appropriate drive and directory. If you installed the files to the default directory, the files will be located in the C:\COUPLES directory. Three directories should appear; Brochures, Exercises, and Forms. If you do not see a list of files in each directory (Brochures will be in the format broc plus page number.doc., Exercises will be ex followed by chapter number and exercise number.doc, and Forms wil be form plus the page number), you need to select **WORD DOCUMENT (*.DOC)** under **Files of Type.** Double click on the file you want to open. Edit the file according to your needs.

Printing Files

If you want to print the files, select **File, Print** from the pull-down menu.

Saving Files

When you have finished editing a file, you should save it under a new file name by selecting **File, Save As** from the pull-down menu.

User Assistance

If you need assistance with installation or if you have a damaged disk, please contact Wiley Technical Support at:

Phone: (212) 850–6753
Fax: (212) 850–6800 (Attention: Wiley Technical Support)
Email: techhelp@wiley.com

To place additional orders or to request information about other Wiley products, please call (800) 225-5945.

For information about the disk see the **Disk Information** section on page **207.**